FOURTH EDITION

MEDICOLEGAL ISSUES FOR DIAGNOSTIC IMAGING PROFESSIONALS

FOURTH EDITION

MEDICOLEGAL ISSUES FOR DIAGNOSTIC IMAGING PROFESSIONALS

ROBERT J. PARELLI

CRC Press
Taylor & Francis Group
Boca Raton   London   New York

CRC Press is an imprint of the
Taylor & Francis Group, an **informa** business

Auerbach Publications
Taylor & Francis Group
6000 Broken Sound Parkway NW, Suite 300
Boca Raton, FL 33487-2742

Library of Congress Cataloging-in-Publication Data

Parelli, R. J. (Robert J.)
    Medicolegal issues for diagnostic imaging professionals / Robert J.
Parelli. -- 4th ed.
        p. ; cm.
    Rev. ed. of: Medicolegal issues for radiographers / Robert J. Parelli.
3rd ed. c1997.
    Includes bibliographical references and index.
    ISBN 978-1-4200-8663-8 (hardcover : alk. paper) 1. Radiologists--Legal status,
laws, etc.--United States. 2. Radiologic technologists--Legal status, laws,
etc.--United States. 3. Radiologists--Malpractice--United States. 4. Radiologic
technologists--Malpractice--United States. I. Title.
    [DNLM: 1. Radiology--legislation & jurisprudence--United States. 2. Liability,
Legal--United States. 3. Malpractice--United States. WN 33AA1 P227m 2008]

    KF2910.R33P37 2008
    344.7304'1--dc22

                                                                    2008014245

Visit the Taylor & Francis Web site at
http://www.taylorandfrancis.com

and the Auerbach Web site at
http://www.auerbach-publications.com

Dedication

This book is dedicated to my grandchildren

Jacob, Nicco, Jewel, and Gigi

Their interest and involvement with

helping others will be my legacy

Contents

Preface

Medicolegal Issues for Diagnostic Imaging Professionals, Fourth Edition was formerly Medicolegal Issues for Radiographers, Third Edition. There has been a continued concern for imaging professionals to understand and to resolve medicolegal and ethical problems that may be encountered daily. The constant advances in diagnostic imaging have had an impact on the practice, attitudes, and moral values of all who participate in healthcare.

This book is an abridgement in the following areas of

- Legal definitions
- Legal doctrines
- Malpractice and risk management
- Ethics
- Patient rights
- Legal concerns of teleradiology

to include patient confidentiality issues. The reader will gain a basic understanding of the important issues affecting diagnostic imaging and the role of the imaging professional.

Vignettes (short case histories) have been developed to assist the reader in applying the principles of law to real work situations. The vignettes presented are ones that imaging professionals may face from time to time. A few of the vignettes have been developed from actual cases adjudicated. The purpose of the vignettes is to stimulate discussion, to raise other issues, to look at various facets of the questions presented, but not necessarily to provide the "right answers."

Additional information regarding ethics and ethical considerations also are included in this book. HIPAA (Health Insurance Portability and Accountability Act, 1996) privacy laws and updates to the ARRT (American Registry of Radiologic Technologists) code of ethics have been provided. Medicolegal concerns with teleradiology are included as well. The American College of Radiology Standards for teleradiology, which will include standards for security and confidentiality of teleradiologic images are listed in this book. I anticipate that this textbook will assist the imaging professional in understanding the importance of the legal and ethical principles when performing imaging procedures.

Robert J. Parelli, M.A., A.R.R.T., (R)
Professor
Department of Radiologic Technology
Cypress College

Admonition

It is evident that different courts and different judges will give different verdicts based on the same set of facts. Even the same court, including the United States Supreme Court, will give different decisions when sociological or cultural changes pressure the different outcomes. This should not come as a surprise to the reader. Therefore, an admonition, caveat, or warning is in order. Medical law like medicine is constantly changing. New decisions and laws are made every day. Medical law cases change faster than books can be published. The cases in this text may be obsolete at the time of printing, in light of new rulings by the courts. The legal cases presented in the textbook are developed for the purpose of illustrating a principle, or point of law, or the rationale of the court, which will pass the test of time. The textbook is not intended to be a substitute for legal advice. I suggest that the reader seek competent legal advice when necessary.

About the Author

Robert J. Parelli, M.A., A.R.R.T., (R), is a graduate of California State University/Long Beach and holds both a Bachelor of Arts and Master of Arts in Education. He is presently the program director for the Radiologic Technology Program at Cypress College (Cypress, California) and holds the academic rank of professor. He has taught radiology science for 28 years and has authored the following books: *Radiologic Technology Clinical Manual, Principles of Fluoroscopic Image Intensification and Television Systems,* and *Medicolegal Issues for Radiographers, Third Edition* (CRC/St. Lucie Press). Parelli is a contributing author in *Fuchs's Radiographic Exposure, Processing and Quality Control, Seventh Edition* (Charles C. Thomas Publishers), and is an active member of the American Society of Radiologic Technologists and the Association of Educators in Radiology Science.

Chapter 1

Legal Definitions

Upon completion of Chapter 1, the reader will be able to:

1. Define intentional torts.
2. Differentiate between assault and battery.
3. Recognize false imprisonment issues.
4. Discuss invasion of privacy situations.
5. Explain libel and slander.
6. Define unintentional misconduct and discuss the concepts of:
    1. Duty
    2. Breach of care
    3. Cause
    4. Injury

7. Recognize malpractice situations.

Legal Definitions

Radiographers complete the work assigned each day without thinking about situations that could result in legal actions taken against them or against the health facility in which they work. As consumers become more aware of the standards of care they should be receiving and are cognizant of seeking legal compensation when they do not receive an acceptable standard of care, radiographers must become knowledgeable of legal definitions of the standard of care.

The law that governs the relationships between individuals is known as civil law. The type of law that governs the rights between individuals in noncriminal actions is called torts. Torts are not easy to define, but a basic distinction is that they are violations of civil, as opposed to criminal, law. Tort law is personal injury law. The act may be malicious and intentional, or it may be the result of negligence and disregard for the rights of others. Torts include those conditions whereby the law allows for compensation to be paid an individual when that individual is damaged or injured by another. There are two types of torts: those resulting from intentional action and those resulting from unintentional action.

Intentional Torts

There are several situations in which a tort action can be taken against the health professional because of some deliberate action. Intentional tort includes: (1) civil assault, (2) civil battery, (3) false imprisonment, (4) libel and slander, and (5) invasion of privacy.

Assault

Assault is defined as threatening to perform intentional injury and/or bodily harm to another by administration of poison, anesthetics, narcotics, or willful and wrongful blows with weapons or other instruments. Assault is the *threat* of touching in an injurious way. If the patient feels threatened and has cause to believe that he or she will be touched in a harmful manner, there may be justification for a charge of assault. To avoid this, it is absolutely essential that the radiographer explain what is going to happen during an examination and reassure the patient in any situation where the threat of harm may be an issue. Never use threats in an effort to gain the patient's cooperation. This applies to working with children as well as with adults. A tort of civil assault can be filed if a patient is apprehensive of injury by the imprudent conduct of the radiographer. If found guilty, the radiographer could be held liable or responsible to provide financial compensation to the patient for damages that may have resulted from any apprehension.

Battery

Battery consists of touching a person without permission. Again, a clear explanation of what is to be done is essential. If the patient refuses to be touched, that wish must be respected. Actually, battery implies that the touch is a willful act to harm or provoke, but even the most well-intentioned touch may fall into this category if the patient has expressly forbidden it. This should not prevent the radiographer from placing a reassuring hand on the patient's shoulder, as long as the patient has not forbidden it, when there is no intent to harm or to invade the patient's privacy. On the other hand, a radiograph taken against the patient's will, or on the wrong patient, could be construed as battery. This emphasizes the need for consistently double checking patient identification. If a patient has refused a particular hypodermic injection and the nurse approaches the patient and attempts to administer the medication, it would be an assault. If the nurse administers the rejected hypodermic injection, it could be considered battery. The battery is an assault carried out or completed. Therefore, the patient must be conscious for an assault to occur. An unconscious patient may be the victim of battery.

There are certain circumstances where an individual committing battery will not be liable for the battery. These are situations in which the conduct is said to be "privileged." For example, a radiographer restraining a patient who is obviously about to strike or injure other patients and/or himself. The action of the radiographer to protect other patients and their interests outweighs the damage that may be sustained by restraining the patient and his interest.

Vignette 1

Assault and Battery

A student and a staff radiographer were requested to perform an intravenous pyelogram on a 58-year-old woman with hypertension. The staff radiographer, who was the department clown, ordered the student technologist to load two 50 cc syringes, one with contrast media, the other syringe with isopropyl alcohol. The staff radiographer left the x-ray suite, leaving the student with the patient. The radiologist came into the room and grabbed one of the syringes without checking the empty contrast media vial. The radiologist injected the patient; upon completion of the injection, the patient immediately became comatose. The patient was sent to the Intensive Care Unit. Blood chemistry, ordered later, indicated that the patient had a high concentration of alcohol in her blood. The radiologist was notified of the blood chemistry report by the patient's attending physician. The radiologist questioned both the staff radiographer and the student. The student told the radiologist that he was ordered to load two syringes, one with contrast media, the other with isopropyl alcohol.

Who would be held liable for assault and/or battery?

Answer

In any radiologic technology program, the student is under the guidance and direction of the radiology department personnel. The staff radiographer could be held liable for assault on the patient and the radiologist could be held liable for battery. The radiologist failed to check the contents of the syringe by asking the student which one had contrast media or checking the empty vial for the type of contrast and amount of concentration. The student would not be held liable because he was directed by the staff radiographer to load the two syringes with two different types of liquid. However, it is important to note that students should not be naive with regards to the types of contrast media used for certain radiographic procedures. The student should have informed the radiologist of the contents of both syringes prior to injection.

False Imprisonment

False imprisonment is the intentional confinement without authorization by one who physically constricts a person using force, threat of force, or confining clothing or structures. It becomes an issue when the patient wishes to leave and is not allowed to do so. Inappropriate use of physical restraints may also constitute false imprisonment. The confinement must be intentional and without legal justification. Freedom from unlawful restraint is a right protected by law. If the patient is improperly restrained, the law allows redress in the form of tort damages. The proof of all the elements of false imprisonment must be established in order to support the occurrence of an illegal act. In situations where patients are a danger to themselves or to others, they may be restrained. A situation where false imprisonment may arise is when a radiographer uses a brat-board, which is a radiographic term used to describe a pediatric immobilization device, to restrain a child and does not tell the parents the reason for the restraint (Ward, 1985, p. 2).

Libel and Slander

Libel is the written defamation of character, while oral defamation is termed slander. These are torts that affect the reputation and good name of another. The basic element of the tort of defamation is that the oral or written communication is made to another person other than the one who is being defamed. The law does recognize certain relationships that require an individual be allowed to speak without fear of being sued for defamation of character. For example, radiology department supervisors, who must evaluate employees or give references regarding an employee's work, have a qualified privilege.

Radiographers can protect themselves from this civil tort by using caution when conversing within the hearing distance of patients.

Invasion of Privacy

Invasion of privacy charges may result when confidentiality of information has not been maintained or when the patient's body has been improperly and unnecessarily exposed or touched. Protection of the patient's modesty is vitally important when performing radiographic procedures.

Vignette 2

Libel, Slander, Invasion of Privacy

A 16-year-old female was admitted through the emergency room with lower abdominal pain. The patient was transported to the x-ray department for an abdominal series. The orderly noticed on the x-ray request form, under "pertinent clinical information," the abbreviation PID. The orderly asked the staff radiographer what PID meant. The radiographer jokingly told the orderly that the patient had syphilis and ordered the orderly to wrap her up, as in an isolation procedure for a communicable disease. The patient asked the orderly why she was being wrapped up with sheets and why the orderly was putting on gloves, mask, and an isolation gown. The orderly told the patient that she had pelvic inflammatory disease (PID) syphilis, a communicable disease. On the way back to the x-ray department, the orderly sent a note to his friend in the central service department that a young female patient, who happens to be in the same high school class, had been admitted into the hospital with syphilis. Meanwhile, the young female patient became very distressed and told her father what the orderly had said to her. The father immediately contacted her attending physician to find out whether the daughter had syphilis. The doctor told the father that it was a mistake and that the orderly was wrong in telling the young girl that she had the disease. Not long after the girl was discharged from the hospital, the father filed a civil suit against the hospital for defamation of character.

Who, if anyone, was liable for slander? Libel? Why? Was the young female patient's privacy invaded?

Answer

The radiographer was liable for slander because he told the orderly (a second party) that the patient had syphilis, which was untrue. The patient became emotionally troubled when the orderly told her that she had the disease. The orderly was held liable for libel because the written note that he sent to his friend in central services was defamatory. It is important to note that any information on the patient's chart, x-ray request form, or x-ray film is confidential information and not intended to be exposed to any other persons. Therefore, the young female patient's privacy had been invaded.

Unintentional Misconduct (Negligence)

Whenever a radiographer unintentionally causes injury to a patient, it may be determined that a negligent act has been committed. Negligence refers to the neglect or omission of reasonable care or caution. The standard of reasonable care is based on the "doctrine of the reasonably prudent man." This standard requires that a person perform as any reasonable man of ordinary prudence (with comparable education and skill) would perform under similar circumstances. In the relationship between a professional person and a patient or client, there is an implied contract to provide reasonable care. An act of negligence in the context of such a relationship is defined as *malpractice*.

Negligence, as used in malpractice law, is not necessarily the same as *carelessness*. A person's conduct can be held negligent, in the legal sense, if a person acts carefully. For example, if a radiographer attempts a procedure for which he/she has had no prior training and does it carefully, the conduct, nevertheless, can be deemed negligent if harm results to the patient because the radiographer attempted the procedure without having had previous training and/or experience.

For a radiographer to be found negligent in court and held liable for damages, the civil proceedings must establish the following elements:

1. **Duty** expected of the radiographer (standard of care)
2. **Breach** of duty by the radiographer
3. **Cause** of injury is due to the radiographer's negligence
4. **Injury** to the patient actually occurred

The courts will interview experts in the field or workers in an occupation to determine if the proper standard of care has been followed.

Duty (Standard of Care)

If a physician instructs radiographer Parelli to radiograph patient Shaw's *right* leg, Parelli has a duty to properly radiograph Shaw's right leg. When Parelli images Shaw's right leg, Parelli will have performed as a reasonable and prudent radiographer would have acted under similar circumstances. However, if Parelli images Shaw's *left* leg, Parelli is breaching the standard of care by failing to follow the physician's directions.

Breach of Care

What if Parelli's radiographs of Shaw's right leg were not adequate to provide a diagnosis? The radiographer has a duty to ensure that radiographs are clear and have the highest quality for the physician's diagnosis. If they are not, then Parelli's inadequate radiographs are a breach of the radiographer's duty. If Shaw's condition deteriorates because the physician could not properly interpret the radiograph, then Shaw would have grounds to sue the physician and Parelli. This would be resolved in court with the assistance of expert witnesses and by the judgment of a jury on a case-by-case basis.

Cause

Radiographer's negligence is the direct cause of the patient's injury. The radiographer has the duty to make sure that a dizzy or semiconscious patient does not fall from the x-ray table. It would be a breach of duty if the radiographer left the x-ray room. Leaving the room would be closely related to the patient's falling from the table.

Injury

The patient must sustain actual injury. If a patient falls from the x-ray table because the radiographer leaves the room, but the patient is not injured, the patient cannot expect to receive compensation for nonexistent injuries. A personal injury or tort will not be successful in establishing liability if there are no damages.

To determine if negligence exists, the court will determine if a "reasonable man" could have anticipated the harmful results. A reasonable man is defined as a man of average prudence, using ordinary care and skill, providing a standard of care or a standard of behavior. The court will interview experts in the field or workers in an occupation to determine if the proper standard of care had been followed.

A duty to protect another is proportional to the risk or hazard of a particular activity. A person is negligent when, without intending any harm or wrong, he/she does such an act or omits to take the necessary precautions that, under ordinary circumstances, he/she ought to reasonably foresee that this act could thereby expose the interest of another to unreasonable risk or harm. A standard of care requires each person to conduct himself/herself as an average, "reasonable" person would in similar circumstances.

Proximate or legal cause must show a connection between the act and the resultant injury or harm. A cause–effect relationship must exist, and the cause must be substantial enough to lead reasonable men to conclude it is indeed the cause of harm. A plaintiff cannot recover unless actual injury is suffered and the plaintiff is able to show actual loss or damages resulting from the defendant's act.

The common defenses against negligence are

1. Contributory negligence
2. Comparative negligence
3. Assumption of risk

Contributory negligence is a situation where the patient failed to act as a reasonable and prudent person and this negligence contributed to the injury. Comparative negligence occurs when the plaintiff's fault is equal to that of the defendant's. Some states allow for degrees of negligence and may allow recovery based on the relative degree of fault.

Assumption of risk is when the patient or plaintiff by expressed or implied consent, or agreement, recognizes the danger and assumes the risk. These legal defenses against negligence demonstrate the importance of detailed incident reports being completed with accurate documentation of the sequence of events, the need of gaining the patient's or guardian's signature on a consent form, informing the patient of the procedure, and giving accurate instructions while performing the radiographic procedures.

Malpractice

Malpractice lawsuits against physicians and hospitals are becoming increasingly common. Legally, to establish a claim of malpractice, a claimant must prove to the satisfaction of the court that three things are true:

1. The patient has sustained some loss, damage, or injury.
2. The person or institution being sued is the party at fault or responsible for the loss.
3. The loss is attributable to negligence or improper practice.

Accordingly, a patient may sustain some loss, but to collect damages the court must be convinced that the loss is due to negligence in professional care or treatment. Usually a determination of negligence is based on whether or not the usual standards and procedures for that particular situation were followed in the case in question. In another case, a patient may prove that someone was negligent, but may not be entitled to a settlement unless it can be demonstrated that a loss has occurred as a result. Nonetheless, it is inexcusable to be complacent about negligence simply because there was "no harm done." Nor should one be callous about the patient's loss, damage, or injury as long as accepted and established procedures were followed.

There has been a great deal of discussion concerning whether radiographers should carry malpractice insurance. Hospitals nearly always carry liability insurance, which covers employees. It is essential that radiographers learn the extent of provisions for malpractice coverage in their institutions. According to the legal "doctrine of respondeat superior" (let the master respond), the employer is liable for the negligent acts of employees that occur in the course of their work. For a physician who is supervising and controlling the activities of a hospital employee, his authority and responsibility will supersede that of the employer, according to the "doctrine of borrowed servant." Regardless of how these legal doctrines may be applied, the fundamental rule of law that every radiographer should clearly know and understand is that *each person is liable for his/her own negligent conduct*. This is called the "doctrine of personal liability." It means that the law does not allow the wrongdoer to escape responsibility even though someone else may be sued and held legally responsible. In some cases, hospital insurers, who had paid malpractice claims, have successfully recovered damages from negligent employees by filing separate lawsuits against them. This would be sufficient reason for radiographers to be protected by their own liability insurance policies. Other radiographers argue that the potential for a large insurance settlement is an incentive to sue and that, if the radiographer has no means of paying a large claim, there would not be a suit. The American Society of Radiologic Technologists offers professional liability coverage on a group basis. The possibility of losing personal assets, such as one's home, may provide motivation for joining such a plan.

A State Can Be Liable for False Imprisonment of a Patient

The state is liable for false imprisonment, negligence, and malpractice arising out of a patient's involuntary commitment to a state hospital, a New York appellate ruled.

In this particular scenario, a patient was admitted to a general hospital for treatment of a gallbladder problem. Her history included emotional problems (suicide attempts) based on marital difficulties. After a series of tests, including consultation with a psychiatrist, the patient was informed that her gallbladder would be removed. Later that same day, her physician told her to dress and pack because he had arranged for her to be admitted to the state hospital. State troopers handcuffed her, strapped her in the seat of a troop car, and took her to the state hospital, accompanied by a female hospital employee.

On arrival at the state hospital, the admitting officer realized that the physician lacked the requisite authority to order the patient's involuntary commitment. He asked her to sign a voluntary admission form, but she refused, protesting her presence there. The admitting officer ignored the patient's complaints and assigned her to a ward without a proper physical or psychiatric examination, and without contacting her family or her physician. She remained in the hospital over the weekend.

In a suit against the state, the patient was awarded $40,000 and her husband's derivation claim was dismissed. The husband filed a second civil suit for derivative injuries, claiming that the wife's involuntary admission into the hospital caused him mental anguish and pain. On appeal, the court said that, for an acutely medically ill person, the episodes justified money damages for false imprisonment, along with an additional sum for the residual effects attributable solely to the negligence of state agents. Affirming the lower court's judgment, the court found that her husband did not sustain his burden of proof (*Plumadore v. State of New York,* 427 NYS 2d 90 NY Supreme Court, Appellate Division, April 24, 1980).

Review Questions

1. A deliberate attempt, or threat, with force or violence directed toward a person by another to corporal injury is
   a. Battery
   b. Malice
   c. Assault
   d. Tort

2. An injury or civil wrong committed with or without force to the person or property of another is
   a. Battery
   b. Malice
   c. Assault
   d. Tort

3. Written defamation of character is
    a. Libel
    b. Slander
    c. Invasion of privacy
    d. False imprisonment

4. Touching a person without permission is
    a. Battery
    b. Malice
    c. Assault
    d. Tort

5. Inappropriate use of physical restraints may constitute
    a. Slander
    b. Malice
    c. Invasion of privacy
    d. False imprisonment

6. Negligence or omission of reasonable care is
    a. Carelessness
    b. Negligence
    c. Libel
    d. Tort

7. For a radiographer to be found negligent in court, the civil proceedings must establish the following elements, *except*
    a. Carelessness
    b. Duty
    c. Cause
    d. Injury

8. A radiographer's failure to produce quality radiographs for physician interpretation would be considered failure of which of the four elements that contribute to negligent acts?
    a. Duty
    b. Breach
    c. Cause
    d. Injury

9. Which of the four elements that contribute to negligent acts would apply if the radiographer left the x-ray room and the patient falls off of the x-ray table?
    a. Duty
    b. Breach
    c. Cause
    d. Injury

10. Oral defamation of one's character is
    a. Libel
    b. Slander
    c. Invasion of privacy
    d. False imprisonment

Chapter 2

Legal Doctrines

Upon completion of Chapter 2, the reader will be able to:

1. Explain the doctrine of personal liability.
2. Examine the doctrine of respondeat superior.
3. Interpret the doctrine of borrowed servant.
4. Apply the doctrine of res ipsa loquitur to the legal case of *Ybarra v. Spangard*.
5. Assess the doctrine of foreseeability to equipment safety.
6. Apply the provisions of the Safe Medical Devices Act to the doctrine of foreseeability.

Legal Doctrines

Should radiographers be concerned about the risk of being named as a defendant in a medical malpractice suit? Things do go wrong and mistakes are made in the profession. In radiology, it might be that a patient fell from a radiographic table or tripped getting into a wheelchair or developed a reaction to contrast media or an embolism as a result of a special procedure. It might be a perforated rectum after a barium enema. It might be a misdiagnosed radiograph that resulted in a delay in treatment or even surgery on a wrong area of the body. It might be an examination conducted on the wrong patient. It might be (and has been) a thousand other things.

The legal responsibility of the radiographer is to be a radiographer of safe care. The various legal doctrines will give insight into the ways in which the law fixes liability for acts of malpractice, and will show how a radiographer may be subjected to a greater degree of liability based on various factors or doctrines of law or legal status of a radiographer's employer.

Doctrine of Personal Liability

If there is one rule that every radiographer should know and clearly understand, it is the fundamental rule of law that every person is liable for his/her own negligent conduct. This is known as the "doctrine of personal liability." This means that the law does not permit a wrongdoer to avoid legal liability for his/her own wrongdoing even though someone else may also be sued and held legally liable for the wrongful conduct in question under another rule of law. This does not negate one's own responsibility.

Although the radiographer cannot be held liable for the actions of the hospital or that of a physician or radiologist, the radiographer can be held responsible and liable for his/her own negligent actions if named in a suit.

Vignette 3

Personal Liability

Suppose a supervising radiographer directs a staff radiographer to perform a radiographic procedure, such as a mammogram, that the staff radiographer is not qualified to perform. Assume the staff radiographer follows the order without question and, then, harm occurs to the patient. Also, assume that the supervising radiographer knows, or should have known, the radiographer is not qualified. In this event, if the supervising radiographer is found liable, would the staff radiographer be relieved of liability?

Answer

The answer is no. The opposite is true. The staff radiographer should know her own qualifications and limitations. The unqualified staff radiographer would be personally liable for performing a radiographic examination that injured a patient. The supervising radiographer also would be liable for assigning the function to the staff radiographer when the supervising radiographer knew that the staff radiographer was not qualified to perform mammographic procedures. However, assume the supervising radiographer directs the staff radiographer to perform a routine radiograph which she is ordinarily able to perform. For example, the staff radiographer is assigned to perform a chest x-ray. While performing the chest x-ray, she pushes the patient's chin up to the wall Bucky device and bruises the patient's chin. Because the patient received an injury, the staff radiographer has been negligent in positioning the patient for the chest exam and causing an injury. Where does the liability rest in this case? In this set of facts, only the staff radiographer would be held liable for negligence in carrying out an assignment clearly within her capabilities. The supervising radiographer has the right to expect the staff radiographers to be capable of performing radiographic procedures without injury to the patient, and he/she has the right to assume that co-workers are competent unless put on notice to the contrary.

Doctrine of Respondeat Superior

The "doctrine of respondeat superior" (let the master answer) is a legal doctrine that holds an employer liable for the negligent acts by employees that occur while they are carrying out his/her orders or otherwise serving his/her interests. As early as 1698, courts declared that a master must respond to injuries and losses of third persons caused by the master's servants. The nineteenth-century courts adopted the phrase *respondeat superior* (let the master respond), which is "obviously founded on the great principle of social duty, that every man, in the management of his own affairs, whether by himself or by his agents or servants, shall so conduct them as not to injure another" (*Farwell v. Boston W.R. Corporation*, 45 Mass 49, 1842).

Simpson v. Sisters of Charity of Providence in Oregon

This is the most involved case of the doctrine of respondeat superior and radiographers. Mr. Simpson, the plaintiff, fell off of a six-foot scaffold, landing on his back, neck, and shoulders. On admission to the hospital's emergency room, the physician on duty ordered radiographs of both wrists, both forearms, AP (anterior/posterior) chest, thoracic spine, cervical spine, and skull. Several radiographers began taking films at 12:30 p.m. They had difficulty obtaining films of the cervicothoracic area and ultimately six or seven "swimmer's views" were done. A swimmer's view is a radiographic position for the lateral viewing of the cervical spine. The plaintiff also had a preexisting rheumatoid spondylitis condition that made it difficult to radiograph this area. As a result "no clear x-rays of the cervicothoracic junction were obtained."

Nevertheless, there was testimony in court that without moving the plaintiff and by making minor adjustments to the x-ray equipment, the radiographers could have obtained a good view of the junction. In fact, films taken at a later date of the area were of diagnostic quality. Radiographs were stopped at 2:20 p.m. on the day of admission because plaintiff's physician believed that the x-rays taken were the best that could be obtained under the circumstances.

The plaintiff was immobilized from the time he arrived at the hospital. However, there is evidence that this immobilization caused lung congestion. For this reason, the neurologist ordered the patient "dangled" (i.e., patient sat on the bed with legs over the side). It was later determined that the plaintiff had a fracture at the cervicothoracic junction and this movement compressed the spinal cord, paralyzing the plaintiff from the shoulders down.

The plaintiff brought suit against the physician and the hospital. He settled out of court with the physician for $150,000, leaving only the hospital as defendant. The hospital's liability, if any, would be based on vicarious liability through the doctrine of respondeat superior; that is, the hospital as the employer would be held liable. The hospital on appeal had three major legal arguments because of their employees' negligence, if any:

1. The hospital's radiographers were not negligent because they were following orders.
2. The radiographers were under the supervision and control of the treating physicians.
3. There was no causation in fact between the failure to demonstrate the fracture and the ambulation of the patient.

Regarding issue No. 2, by a preponderance of evidence, it was found that the radiographers were not under doctor's orders as to the radiographic technique employed in taking and developing films. "There was no radiologist in the x-ray room while the radiographers were performing their duties and normally the radiologist does not see or consult with the patients" (Warner, 1981, p. 28).

The attending physician testified that he did not give the radiographers instructions concerning the milliamperage to be used or the use of grids. In fact, he testified "I would never attempt to offer advice to the technologist" (Warner, 1981, p. 28). Testimony also confirmed that the radiographers must follow a departmental routine, which is based on, and even cites portions of *Merrill*, vol. 1, pp. 218–237, 238–245" (Warner, 1981, p. 28). The court then dealt with the issue of the radiographers' alleged negligence. The court reasoned that:

> The jury could believe the evidence that showed the x-ray technicians to be negligent in failing to obtain a clear film of the cervical thoracic junction and that the technicians were not following the physician's

orders as to technique …, the jury could have found from the evidence that the orders (requested for films) were not carried out in a competent manner. An expert witness testified that diagnostic films could have been originally taken and the evidence that, in fact, diagnostic films were taken at a later date supported this … . *The jury could have found from the evidence that for x-ray technicians to meet the standard of care expected of them, it is not enough for them to take a series of bad pictures hoping to obtain a good one* (Warner, 1981, p. 28).

The Supreme Court of Oregon affirmed the lower court's decision and the plaintiff won. The hospital was held liable because its employees, the radiographers, were negligent within the scope of their duties. The radiographers were not named as defendants in this case, but it is clear that they could have been.

This case is of particular interest to radiographers because the radiographers' actions were held to be negligent because they failed to meet the standard of care requirements for their particular occupation. It was shown in court that, in fact, the radiographers should have been able to secure a diagnostic radiograph. The technologist's inability to get such a film, even after many attempts, was a failure to meet the standard of care.

It should be noted that in this case a radiologist was not present nor did a radiologist make the decision that stopped further attempts to obtain a diagnostic view of the cervicothoracic junction. The court in a footnote even notes that, under more typical circumstances, such a decision should lie with the radiologist (*Simpson v. Sisters of Charity of Providence in Oregon*, 588 P 2nd 4, Oregon Superior Court, December 19, 1978).

The doctrine of respondeat superior applies only when there is an employee–employer relationship and only with respect to negligent acts committed within the scope of that employment. The theory behind the doctrine is that one who is an employer should be held legally responsible for the conduct of those employees whose actions he is obligated to direct or control. Often the critical test in determining liability is who had control over the employee. For example, Barbara Barium, R.T., is performing a shoulder radiograph. She grabs the patient's arm and forcefully rotates the patient's shoulder causing it to become dislocated. Who is liable?

Both Barbara Barium and the employer, Roentgen Memorial Medical Center, may be held liable if Barbara is a bona fide employee and was performing the radiographic examination assigned by the medical center as a proper function for which she is qualified. Roentgen Memorial Medical Center (i.e., the employer) is liable for all negligent acts committed that are related to the function of the radiographer in the service of the employer.

Surgeon and Hospital Liable for Burn from X-Ray Unit

An award of $25,000 to an elderly patient who was burned by an x-ray machine during surgery was found not to be excessive by a Los Angeles appellate court. The court found that the burn was the result of negligence by both the hospital employee (radiographer) and a surgeon.

In August, 1973, the patient, 68, was operated on for a hip injury. While she was anesthetized during the operation, the surgeon manipulated her leg so that it came in contact with an x-ray machine, resulting in third degree burn on the anterior medial aspect of her left thigh. The machine was under the sole control of two student radiographers, who, either because of an assistant surgeon's instructions or because of a misunderstanding, taped the collimator light switch in an "on" position, which prevented a safety mechanism from working and, thus, allowed the machine to overheat.

The patient, a registered nurse, brought an action against the hospital and the surgeon, who died before trial. The patient testified that the burn was still bothering her. She showed the scar on her thigh to the jury, testifying that it caused her embarrassment when swimming and wearing shorts in the summer. The jury found both the surgeon and the hospital employees negligent.

On appeal, the appellate court said the patient's injury was not an ordinary risk of major surgery and that it could have been prevented by the exercise of proper care. "Both the hospital and the doctor were under a duty to guard the unconscious patient against being burned by contact with the overheated x-ray machine," the court said. The hospital was negligent in failing to properly supervise its student radiographers. The court also said that "these technicians were negligent in allowing the collimator to overheat, and the surgeon was negligent in manipulating the patient's leg into contact with the x-ray machine."

As to the contention that the amount of damages was excessive because the patient had no loss of wages and did not have a long life expectancy, the court said that the patient was entitled to be free of unnecessary pain during her last years, and the mere fact of being 72 makes each year of life more precious to her.

Affirming the trial court's decision, the court also pointed out that pride in appearance was not the sole prerogative of the young (*Barber v. St. Francis Cabrini Hospital, Inc.*, 345 P 2nd 1307, Los Angeles Court of Appeals, May 13, 1977, in *The Citation*, vol. 38, no. 5, October 1977).

Doctrine of Borrowed Servant

The borrowed servant doctrine is usually considered when discussing the respondeat superior principle. In the borrowed servant doctrine, as the name implies, the employee is "borrowed" for a particular purpose or agency. The classical example occurs in the operating room. Although the scrub nurse or operating room technician is an employee of the hospital, he is paid and controlled by the administration of the hospital for the purpose of a specific operation. However, that same employee is directed or controlled by the surgeon during the operation; therefore, depending on the facts of the case, the negligent liability of the scrub technician may vicariously involve the surgeon performing the operation rather than the hospital that employs the technician. Here the law infers that the one directing or controlling the actions of the employee has the greater responsibility over the one who merely pays the employee. For example, the scrub technician is asked for a surgical count of sponges at the end of an operative procedure. Assume that the surgeon has control and directs the count of the sponges and makes the final decision regarding the accuracy of the count. If the count is wrong and a sponge is left in the patient, both the scrub technician and the doctor would be liable. This is referred to as the "captain of the ship doctrine." The captain of the ship has traditionally been held responsible for all those under his supervision. Similarly, the surgeon who controls the actions of the assisting doctors, anesthetist, and the technician is considered the "captain of the ship" in the operating room.

The doctrine of borrowed servant can be applied to the radiographer who is performing radiographic procedures under the guidance and direction of the radiologist. The radiologist must be involved in the daily performance of the radiographers and see to it that they perform their duties properly. Radiologists, although present in the department, are frequently not around for some specific radiological studies. This is particularly true when plain films are obtained, but also applies to several other studies including fluoroscopy, excretory urography, ultrasound, CT scanning, and MRIs. Technologists are given various degrees of responsibility, depending on the skill of the technologist and the particular radiologist and institution. The physician cannot, however, delegate his own duties to the technologist. In fact, it is foreseeable that in circumstances where a physician is directly in charge of a case or particular area that this may be viewed somewhat like an operating room where the physician may have a greater duty to supervise the technologist working with him. Such areas might be the angiography and special procedures suites, as well as the CT, ultrasound, and MRI sections. The courts may find it easier to envision that a hospital-employed radiographer comes under the control of the radiologists in the department. In a negligence suit against the radiographer, the hospital may attempt to go after the radiology group or radiologist in charge for indemnification or compensation for any loss.

Vignette 4

Leaving Patient Unattended

A patient with nausea was left unattended on an x-ray table after radiographs were taken. Upon entering the room, the radiographer heard groans and thought the patient was vomiting in the bathroom. Instead, the patient was found lying on the floor beside the x-ray table. The patient filed a civil suit against the hospital. What legal doctrines, if any, would apply in this case? Who would be vicariously liable (*Hospital Authority of Hall County v. Adams*, 140 SE 2nd 139, Georgia, 1964)?

Answer

The court stated that the radiographer should have foreseen that the patient, because of his nausea, might attempt to go to the bathroom and injure himself in the process, especially because he was on medication that might affect his movements and coordination. The doctrine of respondeat superior implies that it is the hospital's duty to exercise reasonable care while attending to the patients as the particular condition requires. The radiographer could be held vicariously liable under the doctrine of personal liability, and the radiographer can be held liable for his own negligence. Patients, on no occasion, should be left alone in the x-ray suite.

Doctrine of Res Ipsa Loquitur

There are certain cases of negligence in which the defendant is required to prove innocence. Res ipsa loquitur means "the thing speaks for itself." In this process, a case is built around evidence demonstrating that an injury could not have occurred if there had been no negligence. In a surgical procedure, for example, it is discovered that a pair of forceps have been left in the patient's abdomen. That the forceps are in the patient is a provable fact. They were not in the patient before surgery and they could be in the patient only as a result of negligence on the part of the surgical team. Another example would be a patient being exposed to radiation sufficient to cause skin lesions, which could result only from negligence on the part of the radiographer. In these cases, the procedures begin with the facts of evidence and proceed to establish that these facts would not have been true if there had not been negligence on someone's part. In these circumstances, it is incumbent upon the defendants to demonstrate that they were *not* the party responsible for the negligent act.

Ybarra v. Spangard

The oldest of the res ipsa loquitur cases goes back to 1944. Plaintiff Joseph Ybarra brought an action for damages for personal injuries allegedly inflicted on the plaintiff by Dr. Lawrence C. Spangard and other physicians and nurses. Ybarra, upon referral by Dr. Tilley, entered a hospital owned and managed by defendant Dr. Swift. Dr. Spangard was to perform an appendectomy. Ybarra was given a hypodermic injection, slept, and later was awakened by Drs. Tilley and Spangard and wheeled into the operating room by nurse (defendant) Gisler, an employee of Dr. Swift. Defendant Dr. Reser, the anesthetist, also an employee of Dr. Swift, adjusted the plaintiff for the operation by pulling his body to the head of the operating table and, according to plaintiff's testimony, laying him back against two hard objects at the tip of his shoulders. Dr. Reser administered the anesthetic and the plaintiff lost consciousness. When he awoke early the following morning, he was in his hospital room attended by defendant nurse Thompson, the special nurse, and another nurse, who was not made a defendant.

When the plaintiff awoke, he felt a sharp pain about halfway between his neck and the point of his right shoulder. He was given diathermy treatments for the pain, but it spread down his arm and he developed paralysis and atrophy of the muscles about the shoulder.

The plaintiff sued all physicians and nurses involved in his case (all but for one), and he sued the physician-owner of the hospital. At trial court in California, judgment was made in favor of the defendant and the plaintiff appealed the decision. The appeal was made before the Supreme Court of California. The Supreme Court reversed the decision finding for the plaintiff. A finding for the plaintiff means that the court found all defendants jointly and severally liable for the damages done. But, it is obvious from the facts that all defendants were not equally culpable. Surely not all defendants caused the injury. It could have been one person, two, or more. But, certainly the gunshot approach used in naming defendants included some "innocent" parties with whomever was "guilty." In fact, in testimony "each testified that while he was present he saw nothing occur." How could the court reach such a seemingly unfair result?

The legal theory upon which Ybarra was presented was negligence, including the doctrine of res ipsa loquitur. Application of the doctrine of res ipsa is relatively recent. The classic example is a sponge or forceps left in an abdomen following surgery. The result is such that it would not have occurred but for some negligence. No expert testimony is necessary; laymen know that, if properly conducted, such results do not occur (Warner, 1981, p. 28).

To apply the doctrine of res ipsa loquitur, certain conditions must be met:

1. The accident would not have occurred if reasonable care were used.
2. The instrumentality must be under the exclusive control of the defendant(s).
3. The plaintiff did not contribute in some way to the accident.

The decision in Ybarra was precedent setting on its facts because no one ever found out "who did the dastardly deed." It is now virtually the standard analysis today. This decision and others like it encourage plaintiffs to use the shotgun approach in naming defendants.

There are a number of reasons why a plaintiff's attorney may want to name a radiographer in a res ipsa loquitur case:

1. To meet the elements of res ipsa as discussed in the Ybarra case.
2. When the "big pocket" hospital or physicians are unavailable, various immunities are applied to the hospital, or because the radiographer was not, in fact, controlled by the physician.
3. When the hospital and/or physician cannot be sued as a defendant because they were *not* directly negligent, nor can vicarious liability be applied.
4. When it is desirable due to trial tactics, such as the plaintiff being able to require deposition of defendants, whereas deposition of mere witnesses is voluntary.
5. To place pressure on the radiographer to encourage his/her pretrial testimony and in-court testimony as a witness.
6. When it is *presumed* by the plaintiff that, in fact, the radiographer has assets or insurance.
7. When it aids or is essential to the case.

Res Ipsa Loquitur Instruction Proper in Suit against Surgeon Who Cut Bladder

In a malpractice action by a patient whose bladder was inadvertently cut during an exploratory laparotomy, the New Jersey Supreme Court ruled that the trial court should have instructed the jury on the res ipsa loquitor doctrine.

The 36-year-old patient, a registered nurse, had a history of gynecological and urinary problems. She had a urethrocele and rectocele surgically corrected in 1973, and following complaints of profuse vaginal bleeding, she underwent a total abdominal hysterectomy on March 31, 1975. A few days later, she developed pain in the right side of her abdomen radiating into the groin and thigh. An exploratory laparotomy was recommended because an unexplained mass was discovered in the right lower quadrant of her abdomen.

During the laparotomy, the surgeon cut into her bladder by mistake. The bladder was not in its normal position and it was under a substantial amount of scar tissue from previous operations. Bleeding and a urinary fistula developed, and at the time of trial in July 1978, she suffered recurrent infections, burning, chronic cystitis, and muscle spasms. In a malpractice action against the operating surgeon, a trial court concluded that she failed to establish by expert testimony that the physician was negligent. The decision was affirmed on appeal.

Reversing the lower court, the Supreme Court said that expert medical testimony established sufficient direct proof of the surgeon's negligence to support a jury verdict on liability. There was expert testimony that it was common knowledge within the medical community that cutting the bladder did not ordinarily occur in the absence of the surgeon's negligence. "This testimony was sufficient to support a jury instruction on res ipsa loquitur, which the trial court did not give," the Supreme Court said (*Bucklew v. Grossbard*, 425 A.2d 1150 New Jersey Supreme Court, October 14, 1981, in *The Citation*, 44(9), February 15, 1982).

Hospital Patient Awarded $1290 for X-Ray Injury

A jury award of $1290 went to a patient on whom a fluoroscopic spot film device fell. A Texas Appellate Court upheld the award.

The patient was undergoing x-ray examination on April 18, 1974, when the cable supporting the device broke and fell on him. He sued the hospital, the radiologist, and others. The patient claimed that the device caused injury to his back. A jury awarded him $786 for loss of past earnings and $504 for past physical pain and suffering. The jury found no loss of future earning capacity and no compensable loss of future pain and suffering. The patient appealed on the grounds of inadequacy of the verdict.

Affirming the decision, the appellate court said that the evidence supported the findings of the trial court. There was testimony that the patient complained of leg pain, not back pain, after the accident. A physician testified that the patient had complained of a back injury before the accident. The patient did not see a physician for 18 days after the injury, and it was more than a month before he first complained of back pain to his physician. A neurosurgeon described his symptoms as nonphysiological and his physician noted a back brace he prescribed looked unused six months later. "Further, in the two years after the accident, the patient made considerably more money than in the year of the accident and the previous year," the court said (*Partida v. Park North General Hospital* 592 SW 2d 38 Texas Court of Civil Appeals, November 15, 1978, in *The Citation*, 40(5), December 15, 1979).

Vignette 5

Negligence Found in Patient's Fall from X-Ray Table

A Hawaii Appellate Court ruled that a university was obligated to indemnify a medical clinic for the negligence of a university employee working at the clinic.

A patient was admitted to the clinic for a barium enema. A university student, acting under the general supervision of the clinic's employees, attached the standard footrest to an x-ray table and placed the patient on the table. When a physician employed by the clinic tilted the table, the footrest detached and the patient fell. He was severely injured. The clinic agreed to settle the patient's claim for $150,690.80.

The clinic then sued the university for indemnity under the agreement between them. Under the agreement, students in a radiology technology program at the university obtained clinical experience at the clinic. The university agreed to indemnify the clinic from claims and expenses for negligent acts of its employees and students. A jury found the clinic 70 percent responsible and the university 30 percent responsible for the patient's injuries.

On appeal, the decision was affirmed. The university was ordered to pay 30 percent of the settlement amount and $57,913.01 of the clinic's costs and fees. The court said that indemnity was not limited to damages caused solely by a student or employee of the university (*Straub Clinic and Hospital, Inc. v. Chicago Insurance Company*, 665 P2d 176 Hawaii Intermediate Court of Appeals, June 8, 1983).

What legal doctrine(s) would apply in this case? Could the clinic and/or university file a suit against the employee and/or student to recover damages?

Answer

The legal doctrine that applies in this case is *respondeat superior*; the clinic is responsible for the negligent acts of the university employee and student. Although with the agreement between the clinic and the university, the university did pay all damages from the negligent acts of the employee and student, both the clinic and university could file suit against the employee to indemnify the university from claims and expenses for negligent acts of its employees. Students are under the direct supervision of the university employee and/or clinic employee. The student would not be liable for any indemnity claims.

The specter of medical malpractice suits for radiographers is, at present, small, timid, and barely reaching its infancy. However, the possibility of a medical malpractice or negligence suit against a radiographer does exist. It is advisable that the practice of "defensive" radiography is a must. Defensive technology should include:

1. **Adherence to reasonably prudent practice**: The radiographer must be aware that as a trained individual with specialized knowledge and skills he/she is expected, both ethically and legally, to practice those skills and apply the knowledge of a reasonably prudent and reasonably competent practitioner of radiography. The radiographer should become a cautious, conservative practitioner conscientiously aware of what he/she is doing and the possible consequences of his/her actions.

2. **Safeguarding, to every extent possible, the legal rights and welfare of the patient**: By actively protecting the legal rights and welfare of the patient, the radiographer is literally protecting himself/herself. By protecting the patient's right to consent, right to be safe, etc., the radiographers fulfill their own duties to the patient.

3. **Acquiring malpractice or negligence insurance coverage**: Substitute the insurance company's big pocket for the radiographer's little pocket. For example, if the patient–plaintiff is desperate, a little pocket does look better than nothing. Not only is the plaintiff pitted against the defendants, but also it is often defendant against defendant. As long as the radiographer is employed at the hospital/clinic, the hospital will have $1,500,000 of malpractice liability insurance coverage for that employee. However, the hospital may try to insulate itself from vicarious liability by arguing that the radiographer acted "outside the scope of his/her duties." The physician may try to insulate himself from vicarious liability by arguing that the radiographer was not under the supervision and control of the physician at the time of the accident. Or the radiographer may want to argue that the accident was caused by the corporate negligence of the hospital due to inadequate staffing, lack of facilities or supplies, or lack of consultation or supervision (Warner, 1981, p. 29).

It would be advisable for radiographers to check with the hospital administration/physician office/clinic to determine if they are named either as individuals or as a class in the hospital malpractice insurance policy. On investigating this point, the radiographer would do well to see the policy itself, and those portions showing the groups covered, the extent of coverage (policy limits), and activities covered (Bundy, 1988, p. 192).

Doctrine of Foreseeability

This is a principle of law that holds an individual liable for all the natural and proximate consequences of any negligent acts to another individual to whom a duty is owed and which could, or should, have been reasonably foreseen under the circumstances. A simple definition is that an individual could reasonably foresee that certain action or inaction on his/her part could result in injury to another individual. It also means that the injury actually suffered must be related to the foreseeable injury. Routine equipment check is important in overcoming this doctrine.

Routine Equipment Check

It is a basic understanding of hospital care that equipment used for, and by, patients should be safe and function properly. The hospital must have some type of system, such as a quality control program, to routinely check equipment and supplies so that all are maintained in proper working order. It is evident that any reasonably prudent professional radiographer could foresee that harm could come to a patient if equipment is not checked and tested properly.

"The Snitch Law"

Under a new law, stiff fines could be imposed on radiographers who do not report deaths and serious injuries or illnesses caused by defects in medical products. The Safe Medical Devices Act of 1991, for the first time authorizes civil penalties to radiographers who do not report defects and failures in medical devices. Violations could result in fines of $15,000 per violation up to a maximum of $1 million per case. The act will force hospitals to report problems they have been reluctant to report due to lack of time or liability questions.

More specifically, the act imposes new recordkeeping and reporting requirements on manufacturers, distributors, and healthcare workers. Key provisions to the law include:

1. Every healthcare provider is obligated to report defects and failures of medical products directly to the U.S. Food and Drug Administration (FDA).
2. Every manufacturer will be obligated to report to the FDA any complaints they receive, as well as any defects they themselves find in products.
3. A six-month summary report of problems must be sent by the medical facility to the FDA. This is a check and balance system. It ensures that the FDA is receiving all reports from the manufacturers.
4. Failure of healthcare workers to report problems could result in substantial fines.

The FDA has indicated that the radiographer will now be more susceptible to direct liability.

Vignette 6

Defective X-Ray Equipment

Richard Rem, R.T., has been working at Roentgen Memorial Medical Center for over five years. During this time Rem was told that one of the qualities of a professional radiographer is the ability to improvise. He has been "improvising" as necessity indicates all of his professional life. There were often times when equipment was not adequate, but Rem always managed with the equipment provided to him by the administration.

He has been assigned to perform portable chest x-rays on patients in the intensive care unit. The source-to-image distance indicator ruler, which is placed on the x-ray tube collimator, has broken off. Rem is unable to accurately adjust the source-to-image receptor distance to the approximate 72 inches. He extended both of his arms between the patient and the x-ray tube, which is positioned at the foot of the patient's bed. Richard's extended arms measure 68 inches. On the next shift change, Rem tells Sally Sievert, R.T., that the source-to-image distance indicator ruler has broken off the x-ray tube collimator. He tells Sally that the portable x-ray machine could be used if Sally extends her arms out between the patient and the x-ray tube to provide the 72-inch distance. That evening, Sievert received a request to perform a repeat chest x-ray on Ms. Ampere.

She positioned the portable x-ray machine at the foot of Ms. Ampere's bed, and extended her arms between the patient's chest and the x-ray tube for the 72-inch distance. Unfortunately, Sievert's arms, when extended, measured only 53 inches. Sievert used the same radiographic exposure settings indicated by Richard Rem. Due to the inconsistency in the source-to-image receptor distance brought about by the defective indicator ruler, Sally Sievert's radiograph of Ms. Ampere's chest was over exposed and not diagnostic due to the increased magnification of the heart. Sally had to repeat the radiograph causing the patient, Ms. Ampere, additional radiation.

What are the legal risks involved in this situation?

Answer

One important duty of a radiographer is to ascertain that the equipment used in procedures and treatments is free from defects. The equipment must be appropriate for the purpose for which it is to be used. There are two elements to be considered for this particular duty. First, reasonably prudent care must be exercised in selecting equipment for a specific purpose. Second, reasonably prudent care must be exercised in the maintenance of the equipment. If the manufacturer's instructions require periodic inspections or other requirements to ensure optimum functioning, such instructions should be followed. If the radiographer observes that equipment is not functioning properly, the prudent action is to have it corrected by the individual responsible for its functioning at optimum level. The responsibility factor depends on several things: the situation itself, size of the hospital or medical center, number of staff radiographers available, and comparable components. If the radiographer is responsible, in any way, for the equipment functioning properly, it is wise to have documentation of the times the equipment is checked and found to be working properly, or, if defects are found, that defects are corrected, when, and by whom. There can be liability imposed on the radiographer and the hospital if equipment, facilities, and health systems fail to function properly. This does not mean the healthcare center must have the latest or the most expensive equipment. However, what it does have must be free from defects, operating at optimum capacity, and, if special training is necessary, used by personnel who have been trained to use the equipment.

Review Questions

1. Which legal doctrine implies that every radiographer is liable for his/her own conduct?
   a. Respondeat superior
   b. Personal liability
   c. Borrowed servant
   d. Res ipsa loquitur

2. The court can hold a physician liable for malpractice litigation for _____.
   a. Their own actions
   b. The employee's actions
   c. The hospital's actions
   d. Both the hospital's and employee's actions

3. If a radiographer was found to commit a negligent act, the court, under proper circumstances, could find the hospital, the physician, and the _____ liable.
   a. Plaintiff
   b. Patient
   c. Lawyer
   d. Supervising physician

4. If a radiographer follows hospital policy, but that policy was found by the court to be, in itself, a negligent one, this would probably result in the radiographer being regarded by the court as acting _____.
   a. Within the general standard of care
   b. Within the local standard of care
   c. Within the hospital's standard of care
   d. Negligently

5. According to the *Simpson v. Sisters of Charity of Providence in Oregon* case, the radiographers were _____.
   a. Negligent because they did not meet the standard of care
   b. Held personally liable for their negligence
   c. Held not negligent because it is the duty of physicians to make final decisions as to adequacy of films
   d. Acting within their scope of practice

6. According to the *Barber v. St. Francis Cabrini Hospital* case, the court found that the patient's burn was the result of negligence by the _____.
   a. Patient
   b. Plaintiff
   c. Nurse
   d. Radiographer

7. The legal doctrine that is referred to as the "Captain of the Ship" doctrine is termed ____.
   a. Respondeat superior
   b. Personal liability
   c. Borrowed servant
   d. Res ipsa loquitur

Chapter 3

Anatomy of a Malpractice Trial

Upon completion of Chapter 3, the reader will be able to:

1. Discuss the concepts of a trial procedure.
2. Report on the function of the jury.
3. Identify the types of evidence that can be introduced to the court.
4. Define subpoena and subpoena duces tecum.
5. Construct a trial sequence.
6. Discuss proper courtroom protocol.

Anatomy of a Malpractice Trial

A civil suit begins with the filing of a petition or complaint in a court that has jurisdiction over the parties. Usually a sheriff delivers the complaint to the defendant who must file an answer with the court responding to each allegation within the time specified, generally 21 days.

If you receive a complaint (a summons naming you as a defendant), your first step is to contact your professional insurer. The insurer will assign an attorney to investigate and defend the suit. If other parties with conflicting interests are named, e.g., physicians, each will have a different attorney.

After the complaints have been filed with the court and the defendants notified, the suit enters the discovery phase — a preliminary fact-finding stage that helps the attorneys narrow down the legal issues and expand the liability and defense theories. During discovery, before the deposition is taken, each party submits inter-rogatories — a series of written questions that must be answered under oath. The plaintiff, for example, may ask the defendant radiographer the name of the radiologist who supervises his/her radiological activities. The defendant may ask the plaintiff the names and addresses of all physicians, including the radiologist who treated him/her over the past five years.

A deposition is oral testimony (transcribed as it is given) made under oath in the presence of all attorneys involved in the suit. The main purpose of taking depositions is to uncover information and establish a record that may be used to the advantage of either party at the trial. A secondary purpose may be to size up the witnesses and determine whether they would be effective before a jury.

Depositions are expensive and time consuming to prepare and, therefore, are not done unless the attorney believes important information will be obtained. The deponent, one who gives written testimony under oath, may be a party to the suit, a nonparty, or an expert.

The deposition usually begins with questions from the attorney who requested it. The deponent's attorney then will cross-examine his own client to clarify the record or minimize any harm that may have developed from the testimony. Other attorneys present will also do a cross-examination to protect the interests of their clients.

A person who is being deposed must be as well prepared for the deposition as a witness who is going to testify in court. No one should approach a deposition without in-depth preparation. If you are named a defendant, you need to review the hospital records on the case and discuss with your attorney the scope, objectives, and pitfalls inherent in a deposition. Sometimes it helps to read an old transcript to understand the process so that you will feel comfortable answering the questions. If time permits, you may want to sit in on a trial to hear actual testimony.

During the deposition, respond simply and directly to all questions, but do not answer any question unless you understand what is being asked. Insist that the attorney be clear. When necessary, ask that the question be repeated or clarified.

During the trial, the deposition may be used in several ways:

1. If the defendant has made an admission, that part of the transcript may be read to the jury even though the defendant is on the witness stand.
2. The deposition may be used to "impeach" the credibility of the witness at the trial, i.e., to show the witness said one thing at the time of the deposition and something different at the trial.

During the deposition, exhibits will be introduced and made a part of the transcript. Exhibits include materials such as (1) hospital policy manuals, (2) radiology records, (3) radiographs, (4) radiographic accessory equipment that can be carried into court, and (5) intravenous (IV) syringes, needles, etc.

Preparation is the key word in giving a good deposition. You must have a good handle on the facts involved, but avoid either trying to impress the attorney with your command of scientific knowledge or trying to outsmart the opponent's attorney.

The lawyers need your expertise and you can rely on theirs (excerpts from Cushing, M. 1985, How a suit starts, *American Journal of Nursing*, 85(6): 655–656).

Subpoena

A subpoena is a court order commanding the person on whom it is served to appear at a given time and place to testify. A subpoena is served by (1) judges, (2) clerks of the court, (3) attorneys and arbitrators, (4) various boards and commissions of legislatures, and (5) legislative committees. A subpoena is valid only within the state where it was issued. A subpoena has *no* extraterritorial effects. Willful disregard of a subpoena is punishable as *contempt of the court.*

Subpoena Deuces Tecum — Subpoena of Record

A subpoena deuces tecum is a command for the witness to bring with him/her the appropriate documents, papers, or books noted in the subpoena. A subpoena deuces tecum can imply (1) medical records, (2) consents and/or authorizations, (3) reports, (4) radiographic reports, and (5) the radiographs.

Trial Procedure

The courtroom can be a tedious, as well as tempestuous, scene. Each of the main actors in the courtroom drama has a distinct role to perform. The initiator of the suit is the plaintiff. The one against whom the suit is brought is the defendant. In a civil suit, the case is captioned *Joe Plaintiff v. Sam Defendant.* A lawsuit is formally initiated by filing a complaint against the defendant. It is then necessary for the defendant to respond promptly to the complaint.

Each party presents its evidence through its attorney. Litigation is civilized, legalized warfare. It is incumbent upon the attorneys to represent their client's best interest using every argument, technique, and legitimate procedural device to achieve that end.

In many cases, a settlement is made before any formal legal action takes place. If pretrial settlement negotiations are successful, the claim is settled. A general release is then signed by the plaintiff surrendering the right to any further action against the defendant.

Imaging professionals are becoming more involved in giving testimony in various cases. It is necessary, therefore, to be aware of one's accountability in these settings. Radiographers and other imaging professionals are subject to a summons or subpoena ordering them to testify as a witness to a particular event. Situations in which a radiographer can be called to testify in a professional capacity are (1) grievance procedures, (2) malpractice cases (as an expert witness), and (3) attesting to legal documents, such as a radiograph or x-ray requisition.

The purpose of the court is to "ascertain the truth concerning matters in evidence before the court, and to apply the law to such matters" (Willig, 1977, p. 188). The function of the judge is to

1. Conduct the trial properly
2. Strive for an atmosphere of impartiality
3. Refrain from any act, word, sign, gesture, or inflection of voice that would affect any predisposition toward one side or the other
4. Question any witness to clarify matters
5. Not influence the jury

Everyone has the constitutional right to trial by jury. Trial by jury applies to cases of *common law* and *statutory law*. A trial jury *cannot* be in

1. Probate court, unless expressed by statute
2. Cases against equity
3. Civil cases of admiralty or maritime jurisdiction
4. Juvenile court
5. Paternity proceedings
6. Cases in which there is no indictment

Jury Function

In a case of negligence or breach of duty, a jury has a two-step analysis to make. It must determine whether such conduct was negligent. Once the conclusion of facts is made, then the jury must determine if conduct was negligent based on that same set of facts.

If the jury finds there has been liability on the part of the defendant, the jury must determine the amount of money to be given to the plaintiff to compensate him/her for his/her monetary losses, pain, and suffering. The plaintiff is entitled to be reimbursed for his medical expenses. He/she is entitled to the full amount in money damages of any economic loss, both present and future, as a result of the defendant's negligence. By being awarded these damages, the plaintiff is said to be indemnified or "made whole again" (Hemlet and Mackert, 1982, p. 18).

Evidence

Evidence is anything that serves as a means to make issues clear to human understanding. Radiographs and other diagnostic images would be a very common form of evidence. Evidence must be relevant to an issue in the trial. It is determined to be relevant if it will render some issues more probable after it is introduced. Evidence is relevant only when other facts are also introduced and examined in the trial. The fact or exhibit that is introduced, such as a radiographic image or any other diagnostic image, may represent only one of the many facts that might be required to substantiate a particular issue. These issues may be the computerized tomography (CT) number (the patient identification number and lead right and left markers) imprinted on the diagnostic image. The law of evidence is the system of rules and standards by which the admission of proof at the trial of a lawsuit is regulated. Under the usual order of trial procedure, the plaintiff, who has the burden of proof or of establishing his claim, will introduce his/her evidence to prove the facts to establish his/her case. The plaintiff presents his/her version of the facts through witnesses and documents.

The law of evidence is a development of the common law. In our adversarial system, in order to assure that the jury receives only reliable information, comprehensive codes of evidence have been adopted. One method of presenting evidence to the court is by testimony of witnesses. Evidence must be identified before it is accepted as real evidence; therefore, this means it must be given under oath. The radiologist/physician is commonly subpoenaed to appear in court as a witness providing expert testimony. Expert testimony is only admissible when, in the judgment of the court, the expert testimony will assist the jury's search for the truth. Therefore, the radiologist or expert witness testimony should be competent, relevant, and material to the case. The expert witness cannot render an opinion without the accompanying facts on which the opinion was based. Textbooks are not admissible as sole evidence, because the textbook cannot be cross-examined by the defendant's lawyer or the jury. However, an attorney may use a textbook to frame questions or in the cross-examination of a witness. Generally, all witnesses are sworn in before presenting testimony. Evidence can be composed of (1) testimony, (2) documents, (3) objects, and/or (4) admissions. There are three types of evidence:

1. Direct evidence — the testimony of witnesses
2. Indirect or circumstantial evidence — testimony of witnesses, from which certain conclusions and other facts are arrived at by *inference*
3. Real or demonstrative evidence — presentation of objects to which the testimony refers; this evidence is for personal observation by the court or jury

Using radiographs or diagnostic images as evidence are regarded only as exhibits to be used in the explanation of an opinion. Diagnostic images are considered secondary evidence used to make clear to the jury the testimony of an expert witness. According to the legal case, *Wosoba v. Kenyon,* 215 Iowa 226, 243 N.E. 569 (1932), the court held that radiographs or diagnostic images should not be presented to the jury as an exhibit unless the diagnostic images (radiographs) are interpreted and explained to the jury by a competent expert. According to the legal case, *Call v. City of Burley,* 57 Idaho 58, 62 Pac. 2d 101 (1936), technicians (diagnostic imaging professionals) may testify as to the identification of the radiographs, which include diagnostic computerized images from other imaging modalities.

Trial Sequence

The plaintiff's counsel makes an opening statement, which is followed by an opening statement by the defense counsel. Both outline what they intend to prove.

The plaintiff presents his case with testimony, exhibits, and other evidence to prove and support the allegations or claims. The defense moves for a directed verdict on close of the plaintiff's case. This means that the defense argues that the plaintiff has not made a sufficient case and that all charges should be dismissed. If directed verdict is denied, defense moves forward with the rebuttal, presenting testimony, exhibits, and other evidence to negate and deny the plaintiff's allegations.

Both counsels make concluding arguments to the jury. The trial judge instructs the jury on the law related to the case. The jury retires to make a decision.

Right of Appeal

A party against whom an adverse decision is rendered may wish to appeal to a higher court. An appellate appeal court does not re-try a case and hear all the evidence again. The appellate court considers primarily errors in the law. The basic distinction is that an appellate court generally sits to review the question of law — not the question of fact. It must be emphasized that an appeal will not overturn findings of fact made by a judge or jury, based on evaluation of all the testimony and evidence, unless the findings are clearly erroneous.

Courtroom Protocol

One thing that remains a constant is that the success or failure of an entire case can depend on any one witness. Therefore, the witness's attitude, demeanor, and appearance are critical toward winning the case. Juries are easily alienated by such tactics as contemptible attitude, improper demeanor, or ragged appearance. Witnesses and attorneys alike are expected to exhibit good manners as a matter of course in the courtroom.

Credibility is inherent in the truthfulness of the statements made. However, there are some techniques that can be utilized to enhance one's credibility. The following are considered fundamental to a witness wishing to make an appropriate impression on the jury:

1. Dress neatly and conservatively. The jury is receiving a composite picture of the witness.
2. Listen carefully to the questions asked. Answer questions clearly and calmly, speak in a firm and audible tone. By speaking slowly, you give your attorney the opportunity to object in a timely fashion. Do not expand your answers, do not volunteer any information, and do not hesitate to say, "I don't know" or "I don't remember."

3. Generally, all witnesses are treated politely by counsel, but if an attorney is rude or arrogant with you, do not respond with rudeness or by losing your temper. Remain courteous and polite at all times.

4. Review any relevant documents, reports, and records prior to trial or deposition to refresh your memory. Tell the truth as you perceive the truth and relate the facts of the case. Try not to testify about what someone else said or did unless asked. This is considered hearsay evidence.

5. It is the attorney's job to protect the client and the witnesses for the client. Do not confuse your role as a witness and try to become the advocate for the client's cause.

6. A classic question often asked of the witness is, "Have you discussed this case with anyone"? The answer is generally "yes" because you have discussed it with the attorney, possibly the insurance company representative, and any other appropriate parties. It is expected procedure.

7. If an objection is made, do not continue to answer the question. Wait for the attorney to requestion following the objection.

Vignette 7

New Trial for Patient's Suit against Surgeon

A North Carolina appellate court ruled that a patient was entitled to a new trial of a malpractice claim against a surgeon who allegedly left a wire in her body.

On October 6, 1975, the surgeon performed a laparotomy on the patient. Because of the poor condition of her veins at the time of surgery, the surgeon had to perform a cutdown in order to insert an intravenous (IV) catheter. The patient alleged that the catheter contained a thin stainless steel wire that was left in her body after the catheter was removed. The physician denied that the IV line that he inserted contained such a wire. Before the laparotomy, the patient had undergone other cut downs by other surgeons and later during her illness several catheters were inserted for IV purposes.

After the operation by the surgeon, the patient complained of chest and abdominal pains. She was hospitalized in November and December 1975. In April 1976, she began to experience abdominal swelling. In May 1976, the surgeon performed a second operation in which he removed an 8.5-inch steel wire that was embedded in her liver.

The incision created by the second operation did not heal properly and, in February 1978, she underwent surgery to remove scarring or adhesions in her abdominal cavity conceivably related to the May 1976 surgery.

As a result of her medical problems, she was unable to work. She lost weight, could not function effectively at home, and had incurred medical bills totaling $43,000. In a malpractice action against the surgeon, a trial court entered a judgment for the physician.

Ordering a new trial, the appellate court concluded that the presence of an 8.5-inch wire embedded in the patient's liver, allegedly there as a result of a cutdown by a surgeon, was so inconsistent with the exercise of due care as to raise an inference of lack of care (*The Citation*, 44(9), February 15, 1982).

What legal doctrine(s) apply to this case? Who, if anyone, would be held liable in this case?

Answer

The appellate court held that there was legally sufficient evidence to establish the law of *res ipsa loquitur* and that the physician failed to meet the standard of care required of physicians in similar circumstances. As a direct consequence of this, the patient sustained injuries and unnecessary surgery. The physician would be directly liable in this case.

Review Questions

1. If a radiographer receives a summons naming him/her as a defendant, the first step is to _____.
   a. Quit the job
   b. Notify the administrator
   c. Notify the State Radiologic Health Branch/Certification
   d. Contact the professional insurance company

2. A series of written questions that must be answered under oath is called _____.
   a. Interrogatory
   b. Deposition
   c. Subpoena
   d. Testimony

3. A deposition is _____ testimony.
   a. Oral
   b. Written
   c. Fractured
   d. Interrogatory

4. The deposition may be used to _____ the credibility of the witness at the trial.
   a. Clarify
   b. Impeach
   c. Minimize
   d. Simplify

5. The initiator of a legal suit is called the
   a. Defendant
   b. Judge
   c. Plaintiff
   d. Attorney

6. Which of the following determines the amount of money to be given to a plaintiff to compensate for monetary losses, pain, and suffering?
   a. Jury
   b. Judge
   c. District attorney
   d. Plaintiff

7. A court order commanding a person to appear at a given time and place to testify during the court proceeding is termed _____ .
   a. Deposition
   b. Interrogatory
   c. Subpoena
   d. Evidence

8. The appellate court will consider primarily errors in the _____.
   a. Evidence submitted
   b. Law
   c. Attorney's deposition
   d. Trial proceedings

Chapter 4

Hospital Labor Relations

Upon completion of Chapter 4, the reader will be able to:

1. Recognize the importance of employee–employer hiring contracts.
2. Examine the integrity of organized labor unions.
3. Apply the regulations of the Fair Labor Practices Act and the Equal Pay Act to employer contracts.
4. Interpret the regulations of the Occupational Safety and Health Act (OSHA).
5. Recall the forms of offensive behavior that are listed in the Equal Employment Opportunity (EEO) Act.
6. Report on state laws concerning labor and explain the Fair Employment Act, Anti-injunction Act, and the Worker's Compensation Act.

Hospital Labor Relations

Hospitals differ from industrial enterprises in their financial and social contracts. Most of the hospitals in the United States are categorized as (1) government owned, (2) corporate owned, and (3) voluntary nonprofit associations.

> **Master–Servant Relationship**: An employee is a servant to engage to render service to another; while he renders such service personally, he remains under the *control* and *direction* of the employer, who is designated as the "Master" (Willig, 1977, p. 192).

Radiology administrators constantly find themselves in situations that demand quick and confident action. They are called on to make decisions and take action that involves some legal standing and could cost the hospital or medical center a great deal of money.

A $7 million lawsuit was filed by an employee who claimed the radiology administrator illegally fired him. The disgruntled employee grossed a small fortune capitalizing on the new American way — financial success through litigation. When employees resolve more and more of their grievances before the courts, all kinds of people benefit. Once attorneys find out they can make money on a particular type of case, it becomes very popular (Willig, 1977, p. 185).

Employer Contracts

The employment contract begins with an understanding between employer and employee at the time of the initial interview prior to actual job performance. When the radiographer accepts a job at a particular institution, hospital, clinic, or private physician office, he/she has entered into a contract. There is the basic understanding that the radiographer will perform the job competently, safely, and in accordance with the standards and policies of the institution. More importantly, there is an understanding that the institution will pay for these services, will provide the certified radiographic/fluoroscopic equipment to perform these services, and will maintain the facilities and equipment in a proper manner to encourage efficiency and competency in job performance. There is a mutual obligation on the part of both employer and employee arising from the work contract. Many institutions do not have written contracts. Instead, they have a general understanding at the time of employment and prefer to have the policy statements serve as a basis for contractual obligations. Although this could be considered poor business practice on the part of both the employer and employee, the court could still construe a contract from the circumstances under which both parties were working. It is much easier to interpret a written contract of employment than it is to interpret the oral understanding of two parties that may have taken place 5 or 10 years previously.

Often the issue arises where a sonographer alleges she was hired with the clear understanding that she would perform only diagnostic sonography examinations, or that she would have every other weekend off. Subsequently, new rules and policies are established or a new administrator comes into the institution. Under the new situation, the sonographer is told that she must also perform diagnostic radiographic/fluoroscopic examinations, or that she will have only one weekend off a month. Before the sonographer could be successful in establishing a breach of contract against the employer, she must show that there was a mutual understanding of the particular facts as outlined above, as well as all the other elements of a contract. There must be *proof* of the existence of such a contract. How much easier it would be for the sonographer to insist that the conditions of the contract be met if she has a statement in writing to the effect that she was hired to work in sonography with every other weekend off. It is very difficult to prove anything when the parties have only their memories with conflicting interpretations of what took place at the initial interview. This does not mean that the law will not enforce a verbal contract. The emphasis is on the difficulty of proving what verbal agreement initially took place.

When the employee claims he/she was hired to do a specific job and have certain weekends off, but lacks written documentation, he/she does not necessarily lose the case. The courts will generally apply the standard of reasonableness to the situation. In conjunction with the evidence presented by both parties, where certain points are vague, indefinite, or controverted, the courts determine what could reasonably be expected to occur and generally construe the contract in that light unless there is substantive evidence to the contrary.

It is good business practice to have the various terms of the contract, such as hours, days off, salary, vacation time, and any unusual arrangements as definite as possible. Whenever possible, make the commitment in writing with a memorandum of understanding attached, if necessary. Otherwise, the court may have to interpret any ambiguities. The hiring contract must list:

1. Pay scales.
2. Sick leave policy.
3. Paid vacation period.
4. The required period of work before vacation.
5. Holiday time off.
6. Work schedules.
7. Insurance benefits, including monetary value.
8. Liability insurance (amount).
9. Discharge — a 90-day probationary period for the employer and employee. Reasonable notice to terminate must be given to employer, including an exit interview by the personnel director.

The question sometimes arises from radiology administrators or directors of Human Resources if they are responsible for checking the applicant's credentials, including licensure, registry, graduation, and relevant job qualifications. For example, what if after hiring an individual, it was discovered he/she had a drug problem or that he/she had stolen someone else's license/registry and was not even a licensed/registered radiographer as purported? It is unfortunate that this and similar situations do occur. However, the legal obligation of radiology administrators, personnel directors, and those in similar positions is to make reasonable inquiries regarding the credentials of the individual applicant. The law does not place the burden of doing a full investigation for every applicant for a position. Under ordinary circumstances, there is a right to presume that the applicant's credentials are bona fide. Unless there are circumstances which would lead a reasonably prudent person to suspect that the applicant may be a fraud or may be incompetent, personnel directors and administrators have the right to assume that they are dealing with a credible individual. Most healthcare institutions, like most businesses, have a protocol to follow for reviewing credentials and getting references. If the protocol is followed and is a comparable procedure to other similar healthcare institutions, then, the expectations of the law would generally have been met.

Vignette 8

Staffing

Ronny Rad, R.T., was hired to work as a computerized tomography technologist in the radiology department at Los Altos Medical Center. On Tuesday morning, Rad arrived in the department at 8:00 a.m. according to department routine. Bill Roentgen, Radiology Department administrator, told Rad that it would be necessary for him to perform fluoroscopic examinations due to understaffing in the radiology department's diagnostic area and a decrease in patient examinations in the computerized tomography area.

Ronny Rad informed Bill Roentgen that he has not worked in the diagnostic area performing fluoroscopic examinations in 15 years and that he is unfamiliar with the routine procedures and would not perform quality radiographs for diagnostic interpretation.

What, if any, are the legal risks for Ronny Rad and Bill Roentgen under these circumstances?

Answer

The first issue to be considered is what was the hiring agreement between Ronny Rad and Bill Roentgen. Was Rad hired specifically as a computerized tomography technologist with the understanding or written agreement that he would not be moved from area to area? If a determination is made of an implied or expressed understanding, or a written document that demonstrates that he was hired specifically as a CT technologist exists, then he would be within his legal rights to refuse to perform fluoroscopic procedures.

At the same time, radiography staff should not refuse to go to another area of the radiology department saying they are not capable of performing radiographic procedures for the sake of not performing the examination. CT technologists are basically licensed and registered radiographers and it would be unethical for Rad to not maintain his radiography skills in all areas of radiography.

More specifically, it would be appropriate for radiographers to be cross-trained and rotated through the various imaging modalities (i.e., CT scan, MRI, sonography). In this way, radiography staff can learn and be better utilized. It is the legal obligation of Bill Roentgen to ensure that the radiology department has adequate employee coverage for increases in patient examinations and/or shortages in staffing.

Organized Labor Unions

Why do people organize or join a union? The general reason for joining a union is to increase employee power and to be certain of a response from management. The healthcare industry is behind in employee fringe benefits versus the smoke-stack industry. Other reasons for labor to organize include:

■ To correct any job inequities, such as advancement, pay increments, promotion, and benefits
■ Employee requires job security, pension plans, and healthcare coverage

The 1974 amendment to the Taft–Hartley Act established a procedure for elections and collective bargaining covering nonprofit and voluntary hospitals. This means that all healthcare workers from aides to technologists to physicians and hospital administrators have a right to be represented by a union in determining certain employment conditions. Through union representation and collective bargaining, the individual employee has a stronger voice and more leverage in seeking responses from the employer. By establishing a procedure for collective bargaining, Congress laid a foundation for orderly and civilized resolution of disputes in the healthcare arena.

In respect to collective bargaining, there are some people who think that there will be nothing but strikes and increased costs. The fact is that strikes are the exception. No one wants a strike. It is economically injurious for both sides of the negotiations. It is held in abeyance as a last resort. No one wants to suffer economic deprivation. That is what a strike means to both sides of the negotiating table. Employees will lose wages for the term of the strike, be forced to use their savings, and very often, even if they "win" the strike, the increase in wages does not make up for the lost income. Employers also see production fall during the term of the strike; consequently, profits are decreased. Whether employers win or lose the strike issues, there is always an economic loss.

The National Labor Relations Act allows any group of employees the right to organize and represent the rights and interests of others, whether those employees are unionized or not.

Unfair Labor Practices

Healthcare facilities, such as hospitals and medical centers, are subject to the laws of the states that charter them. The Labor Management Act and the various state labor relations acts prohibit hospitals/medical centers from engaging in certain conduct classified as employer unfair labor relations. For example, prior to terminating an employee, there must be at least three written reports documenting any discrepancies in employment. The employee must be counseled and given an opportunity to improve these discrepancies.

Fair Labor Standards Act

The Department of Labor is concerned with the issue of wages and hours. The department closely monitors issues of overtime. The Fair Labor Standards Act requires hospitals/medical centers to pay their employees a minimum wage. In addition, hospitals/medical centers are required to compensate employees at a rate of 1.5 times the regular rate of pay for all hours worked in excess of 8 hours/day and/or 40 hours/week.

However, if the employer/employee hiring contract documents a bi-weekly pay period, then the 1.5 times the regular rate of pay will be paid for all hours worked in excess of 8 hours/day and/or 80 hours/pay period. *This does not apply to salaried or contract employment.*

Overtime is *not* mandatory. The employer must get the approval of the employee for extra work hours. Care must be taken to make sure that the radiographer does not leave the department or end the work shift if the radiographer is performing a patient procedure.

The Equal Pay Act demands that employees performing equal jobs be paid equally. Many hospitals are sued under this legislation. Medical aides and orderlies often perform the same job, but may be paid differently. In one suit at a hospital, a disgruntled aide sued the facility because of such pay differences. The court found that orderlies indeed were paid more than aides. It also ruled that the pay scale was unfair, but not because the two groups performed the same duties. Instead, the judge found that orderlies actually did less work than the lower paid aides. Because the law states that equal effort must be rewarded with equal pay, the hospital was not violating the law since the judge established that the orderlies' duties were less than the medical aides'. However, while the hospital was off the hook legally, it changed the pay scale to eliminate the inequity.

Civil Rights Act of 1991

The Civil Rights Act of 1991 is a statute that was passed in response to a series of U.S. Supreme Court decisions limiting the rights of employees who had sued their employers for discrimination. The act represented the first effort, since the passage of the Civil Rights Act of 1964, to modify some of the basic procedural and substantive rights provided by federal law in employment discrimination cases. The act provides for the right to trial by jury on discrimination claims and introduces the possibility of emotional distress damages, while limiting the amount that the jury could award.

The 1991 Civil Rights Act gives nonwhite citizens the same full and equal benefit of all laws and proceedings enjoyed by white citizens, such as the right to make and enforce contracts, to sue, be parties to a lawsuit, and give evidence.

Because the law treats employment as a contract between the worker and the employer, the 1991 Civil Rights Act makes it illegal for employers to discriminate because of race, ethnic background, or alienage. Unlike the other federal laws, which apply to employers with 15 or more employees, the 1991 Civil Rights Act applies to all employers.

Occupational Safety and Health Act (OSHA)

The Occupational Safety and Health Act (OSHA) protects employees from employer abuses, and OSHA inspectors are free to visit any department in a hospital. As a regulatory agency, OSHA strives to keep current with the times as is evidenced in part by the agency's published regulations regarding blood-borne pathogens; the aim of which is to protect the employees from being exposed to deadly viruses.

Many changes have been made in the Hazard Communication Standards, which requires employers who keep hazardous materials in the work place to train and inform their employees on the dangers of and precautions regarding the use of the substances.

The hazardous communications regulations require employers to fulfill four requirements:

1. Employers must have a written program stating the company's overall policy in handling hazardous chemicals and how they plan to protect employees.
2. All chemicals must be properly labeled and include information on the chemical's name, what hazard it presents, and where the employee can get more information.

3. Employee training must be provided, which can be as elaborate as an audio-visual session or as simple as an employee consultation session.
4. All chemicals must have material safety data sheets containing this information.

Noncompliance with these standards could result in fines being imposed on the radiology department.

Equal Employment and Opportunity Act

Radiology administrators are not immune to the confusing and unwelcome issue of sexual harassment. They have a responsibility to act on sexual harassment claims immediately. The employer has the responsibility to eliminate the atmosphere in which harassment has been alleged. Complainants have the option of bringing the issue to the attention of the Equal Employment Opportunity Commission (EEOC) or they can go through the federal and state court system.

According to the EEOC, sexual harassment is defined as unwanted sexual advances, or visual, verbal, or physical conduct of a sexual nature. This definition includes many forms of offensive behavior. Following is a partial list:

1. Unwanted sexual advances
2. Offering employment benefits in exchange for sexual favors
3. Making or threatening reprisals after a negative response to sexual advances
4. Visual conduct: leering, making sexual gestures, displaying of sexually suggestive objects or pictures, cartoons, or posters
5. Verbal conduct: making or using derogatory comments, epithets, slurs, and jokes
6. Verbal sexual advances or propositions
7. Verbal abuse of a sexual nature, graphic verbal commentaries about an individual's body, sexually degrading words used to describe an individual, suggestive or obscene letters, notes, or invitations
8. Physical conduct: touching, assault, impeding, or blocking movement

If harassment does occur, management may be liable even if it was not aware of the harassment. The employer may avoid liability when the harasser is a rank and file employee and there was a program to prevent harassment. The harasser, as well as any management representative who knew about the harassment and condoned or ratified it, can be held personally liable for damages. The employer must take all "reasonable" steps to prevent harassment from occurring. If the employer has failed to take such preventive measures, that employer can be held liable for the employee's harassment.

An act of harassment, by itself, is an unlawful act. A victim may be entitled to damages even though no employment opportunity has been denied and there is no actual loss of pay or benefits.

The three most common types of sexual harassment complaints filed with the commission are listed below.

1. An employee is fired or denied a job or an employment benefit because he/she refused to grant sexual favors or because he/she complained about harassment. Retaliation for complaining about harassment is illegal, even if it cannot be demonstrated that the harassment actually occurred.
2. An employee quits because he/she can no longer tolerate an offensive work environment. This is referred to as a constructive discharge harassment case. If it is proven that a reasonable person, under like conditions, would resign to escape the harassment, the employer may be held responsible for the resignation as if the employee had been discharged.
3. An employee is exposed to an offensive work environment. Exposure to various kinds of behavior or to unwanted sexual advances alone may constitute harassment.

A program to eliminate sexual harassment from the workplace is not only good business, but it is the most practical way to avoid or limit damages if harassment should occur despite preventive efforts. The employer should take immediate and appropriate action when he/she knows, or should have known, that sexual harassment has occurred. An employer should take effective action to stop any further harassment and to ameliorate any effects of the harassment. To those ends, the employer's policy should include provisions to:

1. Fully inform a complainant of his/her rights and any obligations to secure those rights.
2. Fully and effectively investigate. The investigation must be immediate, thorough, objective, and complete. All of those with information on the matter should be interviewed. A determination should be made and the results communicated to the complainant, to the alleged harasser, and, as appropriate, to all others directly concerned.
3. If proven, there should be prompt and effective remedial action. First, appropriate action should be taken against the harasser and communicated to the complainant. Second, steps should be taken to prevent any further harassment. Third, appropriate action should be taken to remedy the complainant's loss, if any.

All employees should be made aware of the seriousness of violations of the sexual harassment policy. Supervisory personnel should be educated about their specific responsibilities. Rank and file employees should be cautioned against using peer pressure to discourage harassment victims from using the internal grievance procedure.

eased poor every time she
was assisting Dr. Diode with a radiographic procedure.
Rem told Bonnie Blur that she had told Dr. Diode that
she did not want him to tell any sexually oriented jokes
in her presence. In addition, she informed the doctor to stop making offensive sexual comments to her.
Dr. Diode rejected Rem's objections and continued to
make offensive comments in her presence.

Bonnie Blur, the supervising radiographer, con-
fronted Dr. Diode about Rosy Rem's verbal accusations
of sexual harassment. Blur instructed Dr. Diode to stop
telling sexually oriented jokes and making sexually
offensive comments in the presence of Rem. During
this conversation, Dr. Diode stated that Rem's technical
abilities were below satisfactory and he insisted that she
be terminated from the radiology department at Phan-
tom Medical Center. Within a week, Rem was dismissed
from the facility due to her poor technical skills. Bonnie
Blur did not provide the Director of Human Resources,
Clay Caliper, any written documentation of Rem's accusations of sexual harassment by Dr. Diode. What would
be Rem's legal recourse, if any?

Answer

Rosy Rem was correct in notifying her supervisor, Bonnie Blur, of the sexual harassment by Dr. Diode. Blur
should have taken immediate and appropriate action to

stop any further harassment and to improve any effects of the harassment. Rem should not have been assigned to assist Dr. Diode until Blur notified, in writing, the Director of Human Resources, Clay Caliper, of the sexual harassment complaint by Rosy Rem.

Caliper should have immediately interviewed all parties involved with the incident. Steps should have been taken to prevent any further harassment and action taken to remedy Rem's complaint.

Because Rem's poor technical skills may have been due to the mental anxiety of working with Dr. Diode, there may also be a case for wrongful termination. It is evident that Blur did not manage this discrimination complaint effectively and within the guidelines of the Equal Employment Opportunity Act.

X-Ray Technician Should Not Have Been Terminated by Hospital for Pregnancy

A federal trial court in Alabama ruled that a hospital's possible liability for x-ray exposure to a pregnant x-ray technician did not provide a "business necessity" for terminating the employment of the technician.

The technician sued the hospital claiming violations of the Civil Rights Act. The hospital contended that termination of the technician's employment was a business necessity and that nonpregnancy was a bona fide occupational qualification for operation of its enterprise.

The court found that the technician's pregnancy did not undermine her ability to take x-rays of patients. Even if the concept of a purpose of safe and efficient operation of the business was extended to include avoidance of possible litigation and potential liability to the fetus, the court said, the hospital did not meet the requirement of the business necessity defense that there were no acceptable alternatives.

Evidence revealed that, prior to the technician's termination, two pregnant, white radiology technicians were *not* fired, but that greater precautions were taken and one was allowed to *read* x-ray films during her pregnancy. The court found that the hospital failed to show that no alternatives to its discriminatory treatment of the technician were available.

As to the bona fide occupational qualification defense, the court said that the hospital must show a connection between pregnancy risks and impaired ability to perform the job. The court found that pregnancy would not have affected the technician's performance as a radiologist and, therefore, the hospital could not rely on that defense.

The court held that the hospital's abrupt termination of the technician's employment constituted a violation of the Civil Rights Act and awarded her $7361.76 as damages (*Hays v. Shelby Memorial Hospital*, 546 F. Supp. 259 DC, Alabama, August 18, 1983; also in *The Citation*, 1983, 46(8), American Medical Association). The professional's title was radiologic technologist.

State Laws Concerning Labor

Most states will model their labor laws after the National Labor Relations Act, also known as the Wagner Act.

State Fair Employment Practice Act

It is unlawful for any employer, employment agency, or labor organization to discriminate in (1) hiring, (2) discharge, (3) compensation, and (4) conditions of employment on the basis of race, creed, color, or national origin of any individual. Should discrimination be alleged, a complaint can be filed by the injured party or by the state Attorney General's office.

Fired Worker Can Sue 'Understaffed' Hospital

The State Supreme Court allowed a hospital worker in Orange County, California, to sue over her firing, which followed her refusal to work a night shift that she said was dangerously understaffed.

The court unanimously denied a hearing on an appeal by Gail Dabbs' employer from an appellate ruling allowing her to seek damages on a claim that her firing violated a public policy to protect patients from harm.

The ruling by the Fourth District Court of Appeal in Santa Ana was strongly protested by the hospital, which said the court's analysis would convert "uncooperative, lazy, or arrogant employees" into "heroic guardians of patient safety."

The State Supreme Court's action makes the ruling binding on trial courts statewide.

Dabbs, 50, of Laguna Beach, is a certified respiratory therapist who was working for San Clemente General Hospital in 1983. She said her unit was supposed to have three qualified therapists for intensive care patients on the 3 to 11 p.m. shift, but on the night in question there was only one other therapist, who happened to be new and unqualified.

After officials declined to provide another qualified therapist, Dabbs said that she refused to work and she then was fired. She now works for a healthcare facility in Tustin.

Orange County Superior Court Judge Judith Ryan dismissed Dabbs' suit for lost wages and emotional distress, saying she would have broken no law working in an understaffed ward and could not sue on the grounds of general public policy. However, the appeals court reinstated the suit.

"California has a public policy favoring qualified care for its ill and infirm," said the opinion by presiding Justice John Trotter. He said society's concern for patient care protects health workers from being fired for voicing dissatisfaction with procedures they reasonably believe will endanger patients in their care (*The Orange County Register*, April 1987, p. A-3).

Antiinjunction Act (Norris–LaGuardia Act)

An injunction is a court order to protect labor from abuses of restraining orders from industry. This usually applies during labor strikes. For example, there may be a danger to sick patients who may be deprived of vital services should hospital employees strike. A preliminary injunction order may be issued restraining the strikers from interfering with the orderly operation of the hospital.

State Workers' Compensation Statute

Workers' compensation laws provide for the payment of compensation and medical benefits to one injured as the result of an industrial accident or an occupational disease, or to the dependents of a worker in the case of death. Workers' compensation benefits are paid to the worker even though the worker may have contributed to the negligent act (Willig, 1977, p. 129).

An employee who is injured while performing job-related duties may sue the employer for injuries suffered. Workers' compensation laws give the employee a legal way to receive compensation for injuries on the job. The acts do not require the employee to prove that the injury was the result of the employer's negligence. Workers' compensation laws are based on the employer–employee relationship and not upon the theory of negligence (Pozgar, 1987, p. 176).

Vignette 10

Workers' Compensation Case

Barbara Barium, R.T., was lifting a patient onto the x-ray table from the stretcher. Barium felt something snap in her back and a pain shoot down her left leg. She continued to work although she was in severe pain. The radiology department supervisor advised Barium to go to the health clinic to be examined. Following a visit to the health clinic, x-rays of Barium's back were taken. The x-rays revealed a herniated lumbar intervertebral disc between the fourth and fifth lumbar vertebra. There were no arthritic, degenerative disc changes.

Barium filed a workmen's compensation claim alleging the above facts and claiming that she was injured in the line of duty. The employer–hospital denied the allegations, stating there was a prior injury that caused the plaintiff's backache and disability. The hospital also argued that the registered radiographer should have sought help in moving the patient. Even if the radiographer did injure herself as she alleged, it could have been prevented by acting as a reasonably prudent radiographer and by seeking assistance.

What decision should be made in this case and why?

Answer

The facts of the case show that Barbara Barium was injured while on duty and while caring for a patient. The key test is that the injuries arose out of, and in the course of, her employment. Radiographer Barium followed appropriate procedure and hospital policy following the injury. She dutifully reported the injury, underwent examination, and x-rays.

The purpose of workers' compensation insurance is to protect workers who are injured on the job. It is not a question of assigning negligence or assessing wrongdoing. Workers' compensation benefits should be awarded to the radiographer or any other employee injured in the course of their employment. It is imperative that when one is injured while on duty, he/she always:

1. Report the injury to the radiology department supervisor or hospital nursing supervisor
2. Document the incident by filing an incident report
3. Go the health clinic or hospital emergency room for an examination by a physician

This will ensure that the Worker's Compensation rules have been followed and benefits can be awarded.

Review Questions

1. A general unwritten understanding at the time of employment is considered ____.
   a. Acceptable
   b. Unlawful
   c. Unacceptable
   d. Poor business practice

2. When a radiographer claims to have been hired to do a specific job but lacks written confirmation, the court may apply a standard of ____ to the situation.
   a. Law
   b. Reasonableness
   c. Evidence
   d. Care

3. Checking the radiographer's credentials, licensure, registry, and job qualifications is the responsibility of the ____.
   a. Employer
   b. Radiologist
   c. Chief radiographer
   d. Physician

4. A proper written employment contract should have the following terms listed *except* ____:
   a. Paid vacation period
   b. Liability insurance
   c. Work schedule
   d. Radiographic techniques

5. There is usually a ____ day probationary period for new employees.
   a. 90
   b. 60
   c. 30
   d. 10

6. It would be _____ for a radiographer to refuse to perform a radiographic examination.
   a. Illegal
   b. Unethical
   c. Acceptable
   d. Unacceptable

7. It is the legal obligation of the _____ to ensure that the radiology department has adequate employee coverage.
   a. Hospital administrator
   b. Radiologist
   c. Chief radiographer
   d. Personnel director

8. Which federal statute establishes procedures for collective bargaining?
   a. Norris–LaGuardia Act
   b. Fair Labor Standards Act
   c. Taft–Hartley Act
   d. Civil Rights Act

9. Which federal statute requires employers to compensate employees at a 1.5 times the regular rate of pay for all hours worked in excess of 8 hours/day, 40 hours/week?
   a. Norris–LaGuardia Act
   b. Fair Labor Standards Act
   c. Taft–Hartley Act
   d. Civil Rights Act

10. Which of the following is a court order prohibiting strikes from interfering with the orderly operation of the hospital?
    a. Injunction
    b. Restraining order
    c. Compensation
    d. Deposition

11. Which federal law protects workers from hazardous working conditions?
    a. Equal Employment Opportunities Act
    b. Equal Pay Act
    c. Occupational Safety and Health Act
    d. Department of Labor

12. Which federal law ensures that candidates are not discriminated against based on a wide set of criteria?
    a. Civil Rights Act 1991
    b. Equal Pay Act
    c. Occupational Safety and Health Act
    d. Department of Labor

Chapter 5

Risk Management and Liability

Upon completion of Chapter 5, the reader will be able to:

1. Define liability.
2. Apply the doctrine of corporate negligence to the legal case of *Darling v. Charleston Community Hospital.*
3. Recognize the responsibility of the professional staff.
4. Discuss the Good Samaritan Laws.
5. Explain hospital liability and malpractice.
6. Assess the importance of patient injury reporting and recording.

Liability

Excerpted from the weekly newsmagazine *R.T. Image,* Facing the Risk, August 10, 1992:

> The physician opens the lead-lined door and steps onto the brightly lit hallway. The act and its required effort were harder this time — it always is when one must face the family.
>
> In the waiting room, she sees that the hospital chaplain has arrived. A quick glance before turning to the parents. Their faces are ashen, yet it's their eyes she hates the most. For without saying a word, the

dire nonverbal messages had been conveyed. "No, your daughter is not dead," the doctor says.

"During the examination, however, she experienced complications and she is now in a coma."

What? How? Why? These are questions that demand answers. Questions that will be answered with compassion. Both the questions and the answers will never end.

"She had a seizure and went into cardiac arrest," the physician explains. "We got her back, and now hope that she'll respond further. You may see her for a few minutes. She is on a machine that assists her breathing. We're doing everything we can."

The kidney exam was necessary. Her right lower quadrant pain and work-up tests confirmed it. The IV was established. The questionnaire was completed. The patient's history of hay fever and asthma, as well as the evening hour, called for nonionic contrast. The risks were known. Radiology personnel were ready for everything — except the physician's response time.

The injection went smoothly. Following the initial film, the young female patient and the radiographer were talking about the previous night's awards show. Then the grand mal hit. Its intensity peaked so rapidly that the radiographer had to grab the girl to keep her from vibrating off the table. The reaction tray was nearby, but the telephone was 10 feet away.

"The emergency room is just down the hall," thought the radiographer. "And the ordering emergency room physician knows where we are."

The patient's strength was immense. Her gurgled sounds were worse in the radiographer's ear. The enclosed room smothers the radiographer calls for help.

Then the tremors ceased as quickly as they had begun, being replaced by stillness and quiet. The radiographer raced to the telephone, calling the code.

Was time frozen or in slow motion, the radiographer wondered. How much time had elapsed? Where were they?

Finally the sounds of the team approached. Were they called soon enough?

This story, although fictional, is a concern for many radiographers who are performing radiographic procedures without direct or immediate supervision from a physician. Hospital policy should dictate that the ordering physician or radiologist be present during the injection of contrast media and remain to monitor the patient for 10 minutes. The physician would then return if complications arose.

An acute care hospital/medical center is under the duty to exercise such reasonable care in looking after and protecting the patient. The legal responsibility of any health practitioner is to be a practitioner of safe care. The following legal doctrine will provide insight into the ways in which the law fixes liability for acts of malpractice. Radiographers may be subjected to a greater exposure of liability based on various factors or principles of law, or the legal status of the employer or the employee.

Risk management is the process of avoiding or controlling risk of financial loss to the radiographers and the hospital or medical center. Risk management is a matter of patient safety. Poor quality care will create a risk of injury to patients and will lead to increased financial liability. Risk management is engaged in the protection of financial assets by managing insurance for potential liability by reducing liability through surveillance. Risk management will identify actual and potential causes of patient accidents and will implement programs to eliminate or reduce these occurrences.

Doctrine of Corporate Negligence

The doctrine of corporate negligence means that the hospital/medical center or healthcare agency as an entity is negligent. It is the failure of the corporation to follow an established standard of conduct to which all healthcare corporations should conform in a given situation. The doctrine of corporate negligence or liability is relatively new. The determination of negligence is based on violations or breach of duty owed to the patient by the hospital/medical center or health center.

The famous landmark decision regarding corporate negligence was *Darling v. Charleston Community Hospital,* 211 N.E. Second 53 (Illinois), 1965. Darling, the plaintiff, was an 18-year-old college student who played on the football team. Darling was injured while playing football and was taken to the emergency room of Charleston Community Hospital. The doctor on emergency call on that particular day was a general practitioner. The physician took x-rays and diagnosed fractures of both bones below the knee in the right leg. The doctor reduced the fractures and applied a cast to the leg.

Darling complained of pain continuously. Three days after applying the cast, the general practitioner split the cast. Darling continued to complain of pain. There was evidence that circulation was impaired, and there was a foul odor at the area of the fracture. There were no orthopedic specialists consulted at any time. Approximately two weeks later, Darling was transferred to another hospital and given the care of an orthopedic doctor, but it was too late. The leg was amputated.

The most important issue decided in the case was the standard of care for determining hospital liability. The court found the hospital failed to meet the standard of care due to Darling, because neither consultation nor examination by skilled orthopedic surgeons were utilized, and there were insufficiently trained nurses capable of recognizing the progressive gangrenous condition which resulted in the leg amputation. The court allowed the rules and regulations of the Illinois State Department of Health, the hospital licensing act, and the standards of the Joint Commission on the Accreditation of Hospitals to be introduced as evidence. The verdict against the hospital was $100,000. The physician settled prior to the trial for $40,000. The hospital was found liable under the doctrine of corporate negligence. The court stated, "The governing body of each hospital shall be responsible for the operation of the hospital, for the selection of medical staff, and for the quality of care rendered in the hospital."

Responsibility of the Professional Staff

A physician is an independent contractor who alone is responsible for the exercise of professional skill and judgment. The staff physician is *not* subject to the control of the hospital/medical center. However, the hospital/medical center will assume all of the responsibility for the actions of the staff physician. The governing body of the hospital/medical center or healthcare center is the board of trustees. The board is charged with the right and the duty to monitor the quality of healthcare being provided by the professional staff. The board members must carefully scrutinize the reports submitted by the professional staff and must assure themselves that there is continuous review, analysis, and evaluation of patient care.

In California in 1974, Dr. Nork, an orthopedist, was found negligent in his care of at least 30 patients (*Gonzales v. Nork*, California Supreme Court, November 19, 1973). The verdict was $3,710,447 of which $2,000,000 constituted *punitive damages* because Dr. Nork's wanton, reckless disregard of the patients in his care.

The evidence in the case showed that the hospital, the medical staff, and the staff licensing board never took any action against Dr. Nork although they knew, or "should have known," he was causing injury to his patients.

The suit was brought by Albert Gonzales. The facts briefly were that Gonzales was examined by Dr. Nork in November, 1967, for back pain. Dr. Nork diagnosed a herniated disc. A lumbar myelogram was done and was interpreted as normal. In spite of this and without consultation, Dr. Nork performed a laminectomy and spinal fusion on Gonzales. He complained of pain in his back, legs, and right thigh immediately after surgery. There were conflicting reports on Gonzales' medical records. A November 30 report by Dr. Nork stated, "Patient had done extremely well, no complaints" (Hemelt and Mackert, 1982, p. 33). The nurses' notes of the same date stated, "Ambulated with help for 10 minutes, had to be helped to the bathroom, complains of pain continuously, left leg felt paralyzed" (Hemelt and Mackert, 1982, p. 33). Gonzales became progressively worse and three years later became permanently disabled.

Mercy Hospital where Gonzales was a patient was also found liable for negligence under the doctrine of corporate negligence. The court held that the hospital owed the patient a duty of care that included protecting the patient from acts of medical negligence by the hospital's staff physicians. The words used were, "If the hospital knows, or has reason to know, or should have known such acts were likely to occur" (Hemelt and Mackert, 1982, p. 34). The court held that the hospital was corporately responsible for the conduct of the medical staff. The courts expect the hospitals to have policies and procedures to reasonably assure proper patient care and to take appropriate action against those who do not comply.

Doctor-Owned Hospital/Clinic Liability

There has been a recent surge of clinics and emergency care centers in operation. Under California State statutes, operation of a clinic owned by a physician will make him liable not only for his own acts, but also for the conduct of his employees (i.e., nurses, radiologic technologists, etc.). The law is very explicit about paramedical personnel performing various acts above the legal jurisdiction. A radiologic technologist is not licensed to draw blood unless the individual has the appropriate phlebotomist certification on file with the State Department of Health Services. Nurses and/or medical assistants who have been ordered to perform radiographic procedures without the appropriate state licensure consider this a legal act. Many radiographers working in doctor-owned clinics and/or offices have indicated that as long as the physician gives his permission to perform duties that are beyond the scope and practice, it is permissible. Not so! Any duty out of the scope and practice of licensure is *illegal* since licensure is an authorization by a government agency to engage in a given occupation (refer to Chapter 10, p. 127). No job is worth doing something that could be a detriment to the patient, or to make an individual an accessory to a criminal act. It is imperative to make sure that you know the extent of malpractice for yourself when employed in a physician's clinic/office. Most doctors may not have malpractice insurance for their employees due to the high insurance premiums. It would be advisable to have your own personal malpractice insurance, which can be purchased through the American Society of Radiologic Technologists.

Good Samaritan Laws

The main purpose of the Good Samaritan Laws was to encourage citizens to assist their fellow man by rendering emergency medical aid to injured persons. These laws were passed to protect the same citizens from civil or criminal liability for any acts or omissions resulting from attempts to give such emergency medical aid. These laws vary in the particular coverage from state to state. Some states limit coverage to healthcare professionals, while other states cover every citizen who gives emergency aid.

In spite of rumors or statements to the contrary, there are no reported cases of successful lawsuits against any physicians stopping to give emergency aid. There is still concern among healthcare professionals (i.e., radiographers) regarding potential liability in emergency situations. However, it is evident from the legislation passed that state legislators, in general, regard persons who give emergency care as a protected class. The individual who in good faith renders emergency care at the scene of an accident shall not be liable for any civil damages as a result of any acts or omissions in rendering emergency care. The first Good Samaritan Law was passed in California in 1959. Since that time, other states have followed California's lead to include various categories of healthcare professionals such as radiographers.

Anyone may render aid in an emergency situation, but under English and American law, no one is forced to do so where there is no duty. If there is no relationship between parties involved, then no duty arises. On the other hand, if one elects to render assistance in an emergency, then one must meet certain standards of skill and competency. The essential element or test of malpractice is the "reasonable man test." What would a reasonable, prudent radiographer do in the particular circumstance? If the radiographer responded appropriately as a reasonable person and the standard of care has been met, there would be no negligence. It is the act of giving aid that creates a relationship between the victim and the Good Samaritan and, consequently, a duty arises to render due care.

It is also necessary to understand that the statutes do not immunize one from being sued. But if, and when, a person is sued, the defense of the Good Samaritan immunity would be raised to show that the individual being sued qualifies under the state Good Samaritan statute and is entitled to immunity (Hemelt and Mackert, 1982, p. 51).

Hospital Liability and Malpractice

Hospital liability and malpractice insurance, also known as "patient liability insurance," is intended to cover all claims against the hospital arising out of alleged negligence of any member of the physician staff and/or employees. The usual kinds of insurance carried by a hospital include:

1. Public liability
2. Products and druggists liability
3. Elevator liability
4. Workers' compensation
5. Steam boiler insurance
6. Sprinkler leakage

7. Safe burglary protection
8. Hospital liability
9. Automobile personal injury
10. Fidelity and surety bonds
11. Fire insurance
12. Electrical machinery
13. Radium hazards

One hospital may have 10 different malpractice attorneys in adjusting claims and incidents, which may occur on a daily basis.

Injury Reporting and Recording

Hospital employees are instructed to report any injury to a patient to administration via the department manager and/or nursing supervisor, who, in turn, should report it immediately to the insurance carrier. Failure to give notice to the insurance carrier, in the case of an injury, may be a good reason to disclaim the policy and may make it easier to award damages to the injured party in a legal case. Even when the hospital makes an investigation, and in good faith, relying on the investigation, concludes that there is no liability, or that the accident was too trivial to report, and makes no report, the hospital then acts at its own risk. The insurance carrier may cancel the policy and the hospital then is responsible for legal counsel and damages.

One Scenario

A patient was lying on the x-ray table and had her left hand underneath the table. She did not speak English, so communication was a bit difficult. The student technologist pushed the fluoroscopic tower up and out of the way and the patient's middle finger was crushed under the roller wheels of the fluoroscopic tower. There was no visible injury, and she never mentioned that she was injured. The patient left the radiology department without reporting the injury to anyone. One week later, the radiology manager received a letter from the patient's attorney with a copy of a letter from the orthopedic surgeon who had treated her broken finger. A negligence action suit was filed against the hospital, the student technologist, and the x-ray manufacturing company. Because there was no mention of an injury or incident report from the hospital, the doctrine of res ipsa loquitur applied in this case. The hospital paid damages to the patient of $3,750.18. **Note:** Make sure that you check the condition of the patient at all times, even at discharge.

Vignette 11

Poor Patient Care Causes Back Injury

Frank Filter, a patient at Coulomb Memorial Medical Center, is scheduled for abdominal surgery. In a weak and frail state due to a long-term illness, Filter needed a special radiographic examination. When he arrived in the radiology department, he questioned the radiographer, Amy Afterglow, R.T., about the pending procedure. She told him, rather abruptly, that his doctor had ordered the study and that, if he had any questions, he should ask his doctor. In a curt manner, Afterglow questioned Filter as to whether he wanted the study completed or not because there was no time to waste. Filter agreed to the procedure.

Filter was quickly and roughly pulled onto a cold, hard x-ray table. The jerky movement hurt his back. During the procedure, he was very uncomfortable due to the severe back pain. Filter had asked for a cushion to be placed under his buttocks to ease the pain. Afterglow had told him to just hold still and cooperate or else he would be sent back to his room and the procedure would be canceled. Filter cooperated.

When the radiographic procedure was completed, Filter was once again pulled roughly onto the stretcher. Again, he experienced severe back pain. He was rolled into a cold, drafty hallway to await patient transport.

Time passed and Filter's back pain became more severe. He was experiencing numbness and tingling in his right foot and leg. Other staff radiographers passed him in the hallway and ignored his complaint of back pain.

When the patient transporter finally arrived, Filter was in tears due to the severe pain. When he reached his bed, he told the nurse, Greta Grid, R.N., that he had severe back pain from being pulled onto the x-ray table. Greta Grid was quite huffy and made it clear that the pain was due to lying on the hard table and not from being pulled or pushed onto it.

That evening Filter told his physician that he had received a back injury when he was pulled onto the x-ray table. Filter's physician ordered a lumbar spine series that evening and Filter was diagnosed as having a subluxation of the fifth lumbar vertebrae. Who would be liable for Filter's injuries? What, if any, legal implications or legal risks are involved?

Answer

Because Frank Filter did not have an existing back problem on admittance into Coulomb Memorial Medical Center, there is a legal risk for Amy Afterglow, Greta Grid, and the medical center. Everyone working in Coulomb Memorial Medical Center has the obligation to provide proper care to patients. This includes protecting the patient from any harm or injury. Meeting the standard of care due a patient protects Coulomb Memorial Medical Center. Amy Afterglow was careless in her rough handling of Filter. She should have asked other staff to assist her in moving him onto the x-ray table. Greta Grid was negligent in not reporting Filter's back complaint to his physician and documenting the occurrence of his injury by the radiographer. Coulomb Memorial Medical Center should be held liable, under the doctrine of corporate negligence, for Filter's back injury caused by its employees.

Vignette 12

Improper Communication Situation

Helga Bremsstrahlung, who spoke and understood very little English, was an outpatient at Compton Clinic. Bremsstrahlung was scheduled for radiographs of both feet. After a brief introduction, the radiographer, Paul Penumbra, R.T., directed the patient to the x-ray suite and told Bremsstrahlung to remove both shoes and get up on the table.

Penumbra immediately left the room to get the proper detailed cassettes for the procedure. A few minutes later, he arrived in the x-ray suite to find Bremsstrahlung standing on top of the x-ray table. He began to laugh and told her that he did not want her to *stand* on the table, but, to lie on her back.

In a frenzy of embarrassment, Bremsstrahlung hit her head on the x-ray tube housing causing a laceration across her forehead. What, if any, legal implications or legal risks are involved?

Answer

Patients are very cooperative and responsive to questions and directions, given they understand what is being asked or stated. Therefore, reinforcing the importance of clear and accurate communication between patient and radiographer is necessary. Patients will do exactly what we ask them to do. However, by monitoring a patient more closely, a radiographer will reduce injuries resulting from miscommunication.

Paul Penumbra should have stayed in the x-ray suite to assist Helga Bremsstrahlung onto the x-ray table. More importantly, he was careless in not making certain that she understood the instructions. Paul Penumbra and Compton Clinic should be held liable for Helga Bremsstrahlung's injuries.

Review Questions

1. Regarding the doctrine of corporate negligence, the *Darling v. Charleston Community Hospital* ... case found the hospital failed to meet the standard of ____ due to Darling.
   a. Reasonableness
   b. Injury
   c. Care
   d. Duty

2. The medical staff physicians are subjected to the control of the _____ in the execution of their services.
   a. Hospital administrator
   b. Medical staff secretary
   c. Governing body
   d. None of the above

3. In the *Gonzales v. Nork* ... case, the court held that the hospital was _____ for the conduct of the medical staff.
   a. Not liable
   b. Corporately responsible
   c. Negligent
   d. Careless

4. Any duty out of the scope and practice of licensure would be _____.
   a. Lawful
   b. Careless
   c. Negligent
   d. Illegal

5. Reporting of patient injuries is documented in the _____.
   a. Patient progress notes form
   b. Physician's notes form
   c. Nursing notes form
   d. Incident report form

Chapter 6

Doctrine of Informed Consent

Upon completion of Chapter 6, the reader will be able to:

1. Define the doctrine of informed consent.
2. Discuss the preparation of an informed consent.
3. Assess the level of understanding of an informed consent.
4. Recognize the legality of an informed consent.
5. Discuss the concepts of: (1) who may sign a consent, (2) spouses' consent, and (3) rescinding a consent.
6. Differentiate radiologic procedures that are involved in informed consent lawsuits.

The Patient's Right to Know

Doctrine of Informed Consent

The doctrine of informed consent could more appropriately be called the patient's right to know and participate in his own healthcare. Informed consent is a doctrine that has evolved sociologically with the changing times. The courts have mandated that every patient is entitled to an informed consent before any procedure can be performed. Judge Benjamin Cordozo, while serving on the court of appeals of New York in a 1914 case, established that every adult has the right to determine what is to be done to his body *(Schloendorf v. Soc. of New York Hosp.,* 211 N.Y. 125, 105 N.E. 92, 1914).* Judge Cordozo indicated that a surgeon who performs an operation without the patient's consent may be liable for assault and battery. An assault is the threat to do bodily harm to an individual. The act of doing the physical harm is the battery. It is, therefore, necessary for patients to consent to surgery or medical procedures in order for a charge of assault and battery to be avoided. Consent is the affirmation by the patient to have his/her body touched by certain designated individuals, such as the doctor, nurse, radiographer, and others.

In *Cobb v. Grant*, supra, the California Supreme Court held that a patient must be given the opportunity to provide an "informed consent" prior to the performance of certain medical procedures and treatment. The court stated that in order to give an "informed consent," the patient had to be informed of:

1. The nature of the treatment
2. Any risk, complications, and expected benefits or effects of such treatment
3. Any alternatives to the procedure and their risks and benefits

The patient's informed consent as distinguished from consent is not required for all medical procedures and treatment. In identifying circumstances where an informed consent is required, the Court distinguished between those procedures, which it labeled "complex," and those, which it labeled "simple" and "common."

Radiologic Procedures Involved in Informed Consent Lawsuits

Excretory urography was the radiologic procedure most commonly involved in informed consent litigation. In comparison with angiographic and myelographic procedures, the relative risk of serious injuries from excretory urography is so low that even though the total number of excretory urograms is greater than that for the other procedures, fewer injuries might be expected. The lower frequency of risk disclosure to patients for urography compared with angiography and myelography may well explain why it is involved in a greater number of informed consent lawsuits.

Spring et al. (1988) have reported that informed consent lawsuits involved excretory urography about six times as often as contrast material-enhanced computed tomography (CT). The study suggests that an increase in the number of newer contrast studies (e.g., CT or digital subtraction angiography) may result in an increase in informed consent lawsuits.

Informed consent was considered by the defendant radiologist to be a significant factor in most of the reported lawsuits involving angiographic procedures. In 10 (91 percent) of 11 lawsuits, the defendant radiologist made a documented effort to obtain an informed consent. All but one of these lawsuits resulted in favorable outcomes for the defense. Angiography is ordinarily perceived as having a higher risk of injury than other radiological procedures and, therefore, more frequently involves a documented effort to obtain informed consent. This may explain both the lower incidence of lawsuits instigated and of favorable outcomes for the plaintiff (Spring, et al, 1988, p. 248).

Preparation of an Informed Consent

A physician who instigates an informed consent form should prepare the form by setting forth medical information with respect to the nature of the procedure or treatment, its expected benefits or effects, its possible risks and complications, and the alternatives to the proposed treatment or procedure, and their possible risks and complications. The form must either be supplemented through verbal discussions with the patient and/or through written additions that set forth such information. These forms are helpful only if they can be understood by the patient. Therefore, it is extremely important for the medical information set forth in such forms to be written in clear, simple, and easily understood terms. In addition, it is absolutely essential for such forms to clearly state that the patient should ask any and all questions he/she may have about the proposed procedure. A copy of the informed consent should be placed in the patient's medical records.

Verification of Informed Consent

The physician (radiologist), not the hospital, has the fiduciary duty to disclose all information relevant to the patient's decision and to obtain the patient's informed consent. Further, the obtaining of informed consent involves the practice of medicine in which the hospital and its employees should not intervene. Hospital employees are not licensed or qualified to adequately explain the various types of medical procedures to the patient and to respond to the patient's potential questions. Only the physician has both the technical knowledge and the background knowledge of the particular patient's condition necessary to assure that an adequate disclosure of information, including that pertaining to the risks of treatment, has been given for *that patient*, and that proper responses have been given to the patient's questions.

Hospital personnel (radiographers) cannot and should not be responsible for securing the patient's informed consent (and concomitantly, giving the patient the information that is required in order to secure the patient's informed consent). It can be expected that patients will ask hospital staff who are performing a procedure pursuant to the doctor's (radiologists) orders questions about what they will be or are doing. Radiographers generally may answer such questions; however, if it appears that the patient has significant questions about the nature of the procedure (and its benefits or risks), this may indicate that he/she may not have been given sufficient information about the procedure or may not understand the information he/she was given. The radiographer should contact the patient's physician and/or radiologist in order to allow him/her to answer the questions and, thereby, help to assure that the patient has truly given an informed consent to the procedure.

It must be understood that the radiographer is not the one performing the fluoroscopic procedure the patient is about to undergo. The radiographer does not have the necessary information, nor does he/she know what alternative radiographic procedures are available for the patient. Radiographers should not allow themselves to be placed in the ridiculous position of "witnessing the patient's signature." It is common practice for the radiographer to have the function of getting the patient to sign the radiological procedure consent form. The radiographer, generally, may not be present when the patient's physician or radiologist presumably gave the necessary instructions and explanations to the patient. The radiographer could be held personally liable if he/she knew, or should have known, the patient was uninformed and did not take remedial measures. The hospital could also be held liable under the doctrine of corporate negligence or respondeat superior if, through its personnel, the hospital knew, or had reason to know, that physicians (radiologists) or staff personnel performed procedures without a bona fide consent. The radiographer has a professional obligation to protect his/her employer's interests. Because the hospital has an obligation to see that the patient is informed, the radiographer would be decreasing the legal risk to the hospital by informing the physician (radiologist) of the patient's needs.

Legality of Informed Consents

It is basic that the intentional touching of another without his/her consent could be construed as a legal wrong constituting assault, battery, or both. *Consent* is the affirmation by the patient to have his/her body touched by certain designated individuals, such as a doctor, nurse, radiographer, or others. There are different classifications of consents. There is the implied consent. When a patient rolls up his/her sleeve to receive an injection, this action can be construed as giving consent to the procedure. An expressed consent, as the term applies, is an affirmative action or statement to signify one's intention. There are also verbal and written consents. An oral or verbal consent is binding. The problem arises when it comes to a question of *evidentiary matter*. It might be difficult to prove the patient gave an oral consent. Even where witnesses are present and hear the consent given, their testimony might not be consistent on details and could weaken their credibility. A written consent obviously offers some tangible proof that the patient voluntarily signed a form. It is subject to scrutiny and disbelief if other facts relevant to the situation indicate that the patient did not fully and intelligently understand what the affixing of his/her signature meant in relation to his/her medical care.

A proper consent form is an important evidentiary document in the event of a dispute regarding the claim that an informed consent was not given. The signed consent would generally be considered presumptive evidence that information to perform a particular act was given. The individual giving consent must be mentally competent and able to appreciate the material facts. The patient must have consented voluntarily, based on sufficient knowledge and information to make an intelligent decision.

Rescinding Consent

The patient may rescind the consent given either verbally or in writing at any time. A written consent may be rescinded verbally. Any time a patient withdraws his/her consent, it is as though he/she had never given a consent. This means that any procedure done on a patient who has rescinded his/her consent would be considered battery.

Who May Consent?

The patient on whom the procedure is to be performed is the only one who has authority over his/her body as long as he/she is conscious and competent. The consent is invalid if the patient is intoxicated, under the influence of narcotics, delirious, and/or irrational. It is essential to respect the individual's right to make his/her own decisions. If the patient is mentally incompetent, consent must be obtained from a person legally authorized to give consent for the patient. For example, an elderly or infirm person may have had the foresight to authorize a power of attorney designating a child or relative to act on his/her behalf.

Spouse's Consent

Can a husband consent to his wife's operation or radiology procedure in a nonemergency situation? The answer is clearly no. And the reverse is true. The wife has no authority to consent for the husband.

Minor's Consent

A minor is considered to be under the jurisdiction of his/her parents until the age of majority. In most states, the age of majority is 18 years. The minor may consent for his/her own care if (1) married, (2) emancipated, (3) pregnant, (4) suffering from venereal disease, or (5) in need of psychological or psychiatric care. The term *emancipated* means the individual is no longer under the control of another. Generally, this occurs where a minor is working and is responsible for his/her own support and necessities.

The common law holds that the natural parents or legal guardians of a child have the authority to consent to medical care for the minor. The parent is presumed to act in the best interest of the child and, therefore, there is a presumption that the child will be protected. There are times when parents, because of religious beliefs, will not permit the child to receive medical care that society believes is in the best interest of the child. In these circumstances, the state must exercise its right under the parens patriae doctrine and intervene to protect the health of the child. The law may not interfere with religious convictions, but it may interfere with religious practice. Religious belief is not a lawful excuse for breach of duty to provide medical care for a child. The rights of religion and parenthood are not beyond the limitations of the 14th Amendment of the U.S. Constitution.

According to the Committee of Pediatric Emergency Medicine, state and federal laws and medical ethics recommendations support the emergency treatment of minors with an identified emergency medical condition, regardless of consent issues. Appropriate medical care for the minor patient, during school hours, with an urgent or emergent condition should never be withheld or delayed because of problems with obtaining a parental or guardian consent.

Patient Can Sue for Failure to Obtain Informed Consent

A North Carolina appellate court ruled that a patient's voluntary dismissal of a claim of negligent treatment did not result in dismissal of her claim for failure to obtain informed consent. The patient brought an action against radiologists alleging that they failed to adequately inform her of the known hazards of radiation therapy and, therefore, did not obtain her informed consent for treatment. She also alleged negligence in administering the radiation. The treatment resulted in severe radiation damage to her intestines.

The patient voluntarily dismissed her claim based on negligence in rendering medical services. The radiologists alleged that her claim of lack of informed consent was barred by the statute of limitations. The trial court granted their motion to dismiss.

On appeal, the radiologists contended that the patient took a voluntary dismissal on the question of their failure to obtain informed consent, arguing that "rendering medical services" included obtaining the informed consent to the treatment as well as the actual treatment. The court found that the work rendered applied to performance of the medical procedure, and that the informed consent claim was not voluntarily dismissed.

The radiologists also contended that uninformed or invalid consent was the same as no consent at all and, therefore, the subsequent treatment constituted unauthorized touching or battery. Thus, the action would be controlled by the one-year statute of limitations for battery.

The court found that the claim was for malpractice based on failure to disclose the various choices with regard to the proposed treatment and the dangers involved, and that the three-year statute of limitations applied. Holding that the patient's claim was not barred, the court reversed the trial court's judgment (*Nelson v. Patrick*, 293 S.E. Second 829 North Carolina Court of Appeals, August 3, 1982, also in *The Citation*, 46(8): 89–90).

Vignette 13

Informed Consent

Ula Umbra is a 60-year-old female admitted to Resolution Hospital for a coronary angiogram. Umbra has signed the routine consent form as required by the hospital. This was done in admitting and witnessed by the admission clerk.

During the course of preparing Umbra for the coronary angiogram, Gerry Generator, R.T., talks to Umbra about her healthcare in general. Umbra states to Generator, "My doctor has not discussed this procedure with me, but I guess he will before it begins, won't he?" Generator asks Umbra if she read and signed the consent form. She states, "I read the consent form, but I really don't understand what is going to be done."

What, if any, obligation does the radiographer have toward Umbra? Would he be liable if Umbra had the coronary angiogram under the above circumstances?

Answer

Gerry Generator, R.T., has several obligations. There is an obligation to the patient, the physician, and to Resolution Hospital. When it becomes evident that the patient has either not been fully informed regarding the coronary angiogram, or does not understand the implications of the procedure, the physician performing the procedure should be notified immediately.

The radiographer should document the situation and the fact that the physician was notified. The radiographer has an obligation to inform the patient's physician of the patient's statement so that the doctor may take corrective measures.

Resolution Hospital has no direct obligation to inform the patient regarding the coronary angiogram to be done. In fact, it cannot do so because only the physician knows what techniques and specific procedures will be utilized for the specific patient. However, Resolution Hospital could be held as a party-defendant by the patient alleging no consent was given; the radiographer should take all reasonable measures to protect the hospital.

The radiographer should protect himself, also, because the patient could include the radiographer as a party-defendant. The patient has put the radiographer on notice that she is uninformed regarding her imminent coronary angiogram. The radiographer should notify the physician, the supervising radiographer, and any other appropriate parties of the situation. Otherwise, the radiographer could be held liable if the coronary angiogram were performed without the patient's consent.

Vignette 14

Informed Consent Situation

Vicky Volt, R.T., is a staff radiographer at Incandescent General Hospital. Molly Milliampere, a 72-year-old woman, is scheduled for a lumbar myelogram. Volt is responsible for getting a consent signed by Milliampere consenting to the procedure. As Volt begins to explain the procedure to the patient, Milliampere asks that her daughter be contacted to give permission before the procedure begins. The radiographer has tried several times to contact Milliampere's daughter, but is unable to reach her. The radiologist, Dr. Ohm, states that he has to go ahead with the procedure because the patient is scheduled for surgery immediately after the lumbar myelogram.

What, if anything, should Volt do?

Can Dr. Ohm proceed with the lumbar myelogram? If so, under what circumstances? What, if any, legal liabilities would be involved?

Answer

There is nothing in the situation to indicate Molly Milliampere is not competent and capable of consenting to the procedure herself. The patient may consent or withhold consent for medical treatment or procedure. The fact that she wants her daughter contacted should be respected. The daughter should be notified as requested. Milliampere may wish to consult with her daughter before submitting to the lumbar myelogram. However, the daughter's consent cannot be substituted for her mother's consent. The fact that Milliampere is 72 years old has no bearing on her right to make decisions regarding her own body. Unless there is some evidence of incompetence or inability, only Milliampere can give an informed consent for the procedure.

Dr. Ohm can only proceed with the lumbar myelogram if Milliampere has given an informed consent. It would be wise and good business for the daughter to be incorporated into the consent procedure because the patient specifically requested this, but the daughter cannot authorize the procedure where the patient is capable of consenting. It is not an emergency at this point, and Dr. Ohm could not proceed under the Emergency Rule. He must have the patient's valid consent.

If the above was not done in accordance with general practice in procuring consents, and the patient could establish she did not give a valid consent, the physician, radiographer, and hospital might be sued and found liable for assault and battery.

Postscripts to Vignette 13 and Vignette 14

The First Amendment guarantees the integrity of one's body. Any touching of an individual's body without appropriate authority or the individual's consent could be construed as an assault and battery. The courts recognize assault and battery as giving rise to a criminal action for which the law gives a remedy in monetary damages.

The hospital and its employees, as well as the doctors, can be held liable for performing treatment or procedures without the patient's consent. The courts apply the doctrine of corporate liability, respondeat superior, or other appropriate law and, where it can be ascertained that the hospital, as in these cases, knew or should have known there was no bona fide informed consent by the patient and did not correct the situation but permitted uninformed procedures, the radiographer, physician, and hospital are at legal risk.

There must be some criteria that the radiographer follows to ensure that proper consent is obtained. The patient must be conscious and able to comprehend the document that is being signed. There should be a reasonable belief on the part of the radiographer that the patient has been informed regarding the nature and purpose of the procedure and the possible risks related to it. The patient should be able to read, write, and understand the language being used for communication. The patient should be consenting to the procedure freely, voluntarily, and without any coercion "of his own will."

Review Questions

1. The California State Supreme Court indicated that, written into an informed consent, the patient must be informed of all the following except:
   a. Nature of the treatment
   b. Reasonable response to requests
   c. Risks, complications, and benefits
   d. Alternatives to the procedures

2. The ____ has the fiduciary duty to obtain the patient's informed consent.
   a. Radiographer
   b. Physician
   c. Hospital
   d. Nurse

3. A written consent may be rescinded verbally or ____ at any time.
   a. In writing
   b. By statute
   c. Mandated
   d. By physician order

4. A consent is invalid under the following patient conditions except:
   a. Intoxication
   b. Sanity
   c. Delirium
   d. Drugged

5. Which of the following will allow a minor to consent for care?
   a. Emancipated
   b. Pregnant
   c. In need of psychological care
   d. All of the above

6. California law permits medical treatment without parental consent during ___.
   a. A sporting event
   b. School hours
   c. Babysitting hours
   d. The morning hours

Chapter 7

Ethics

Upon completion of Chapter 7, the reader will be able to:

1. Define ethics, deontology, and teleology.
2. Distinguish between act nonconsequentialism and rule nonconsequentialism.
3. Discuss the concepts of categorical imperative, prima facie duties, justice, and natural law ethics.
4. Distinguish between act utilitarianism and rule utilitarianism.
5. List the principles of beneficence and nonmaleficence.
6. Identify the patient's right to autonomy.
7. Discuss the patient's bill of rights.
8. Define confidentiality.
9. Identify liabilities for disclosure of confidential information.
10. Differentiate between morals, ethics, and law.
11. Describe the Code of Ethics of the American Registry of Radiologic Technologists.
12. Define euthanasia.
13. Recognize the responsibilities and accountability for humanistic behavior in providing healthcare to the patient.

Ethics

Unlike legal issues where a statute or judicial decision can be referred to for guidance, the ethical area is subject to (1) philosophical, (2) theological, and (3) individual interpretation of what is right or wrong in a particular situation.

Distinction between Moral, Ethics, and Law

Morality is fundamentally the inner conscience. Morality is one's concept of what is right or wrong as it relates to that conscience, to God, a higher being, or to one's atheistic logical thinking. Morality could be defined as fidelity to conscience.

Ethics is the principle of morality, including both the science of the good and the nature of the right, or the rules of conduct recognized in respect to a particular class of human actions. A broader conceptual definition is that ethics is primarily concerned with the good of the individual, concentrating on motives and attitudes. Ethical sanctions are internal and appeal to one's honor, conscience, or what is good for society. Every profession, including radiography, has a code of ethics, which serves as a guide for professional conduct.

Legal concepts are distinguishable from ethics. Law is defined as the sum total of manmade rules and regulations by which society is governed in a formal and legally binding manner. The law mandates certain acts and forbids certain other acts under penalty of criminal sanction, such as a fine or imprisonment, or civil action. The law is primarily concerned with the good of society, as a functioning unit as opposed to ethics' primary concern with the good of the individual within the society. Therefore, a radiographer or a healthcare professional, who would take the life of a terminally ill patient, no matter how noble the motivation of the act, would be subject to a charge of murder.

Ethics is a fundamental part of the life of everyone in society and takes a specific form when someone assumes the role of *health professional*. Philosophers and theologians who study ethics try to understand morality in a systematic way. Many try to apply it to everyday problems among individuals, in institutions, and in society. To some extent, we all become ethicists when we learn how to use tools of ethical analysis. The traditional ethical theories are generally divided into two schools of thought: deontology and teleology.

Deontology

Immanuel Kant (1724–1804) developed deontology. Kant endeavored to exclude the consideration of consequences when making moral decisions of performing moral acts. Kant established: Nothing is good in and of itself except *a good will*. Kant defined *will* as the unique human ability to act according to principles or laws. The concept of *duty* is also contained in Kant's theory of good will. Kant based his theory on Saint Thomas Aquinas's natural law ethics, which defined humans as rational beings, with their morality based on a uniquely human capacity to reason.

Deontologists believe that morality is based on reason and that the principles derived from reason are universal and should be held as universal truths. Kant assembled what is known as Kant's Categorical Imperative, which states that we should act in such a way as to will the maxim of our actions to become universal law. Maxim is defined as an expressed principle of rule of conduct or a statement of a general truth.

The maxim, ascribed to Kant that has relevance to imaging professionals is this: "We must always treat others as ends and not as means only." Imaging professionals adhering to this position would never view their role of providing care to a patient as just a job for which one receives pay, but would view each patient as a person to whom a professional duty is owed.

Therefore, deontology is a duty-based ethical theory. It may be referred to as nonconsequentialism. There are two categories of nonconsequentialist deontological ethical theories: *act* and *rule*.

Act nonconsequentialism proclaims that each act or action should be evaluated individually to ascertain whether it is right or wrong. This theory holds that there are no rules or guidelines to govern our behavior; the situation governs the act or action. Each situation must be seen and evaluated as a unique ethical problem. *Rule nonconsequentialism* establishes that there are one or more rules, which may be derived from the nature of a situation, which serve as the moral standards for ethical decision making. While other categories may exist, there are generally four accepted positions on rule nonconsequentialism: the categorical imperative, prima facie duties, the principle of justice, and natural law ethics.

1. Categorical imperative maintains that a rule of conduct or statement of general truth will become the universal law.
2. Prima facie duties allow us to make choices among conflicting duties. A prima facie duty is actually binding if it conflicts with no other duties, rights, or other compelling norms of ethics that are weighed in a given situation. Prima facie duties are intuitive and conditional. The intuition is simply that the feeling within the act or action is right. Conditional duties can be overridden and still retain their character as duties. These duties, as they pertain to imaging professionals, can be referred to as Principles of Biomedical Ethics, which are the framework of the *codes of ethics* of imaging professionals.
3. Justice can be thought of as an *arbitrator*. It is called on when there are problems regarding what is rightfully due a person, institution, or society. Patients do not always get all that they deserve or need, and anyone who worries about that is worrying about the *justice* of the situation. Their concern is that all similarly situated persons receive their *fair share* of benefits, and assume their fair share of burdens. The duty of justice requires an equitable distribution of benefits and burdens. An imaging professional would continue the procedure and/or treatment as long as the patient would benefit from the procedure or treatment. The patient has a legitimate claim to services on the basis of their medical needs.
4. Natural Law Ethics is an interpretation of natural law theory which is a general opinion that "moral principles are objective truths, which can be discovered in the nature of things by reason alone." St. Thomas Aquinas established

that natural law contains rules of conduct based on God-given inclinations inherent within the nature of every human. According to St. Thomas Aquinas, God's intentions for humans are: preservation of life, propagation of the species, education of the progeny, and the pursuit of truth and a peaceful society. Aquinas maintained that God has endowed the human species with the ability to reason. Therefore, when we act according to reason, we act in accordance with the nature of humankind; if we act contrary to reason, it is both unnatural and immoral (Wilson, 1997, p. 7).

Teleology

Teleological ethics are concerned with consequences. The most important teleological theory for consideration is utilitarianism or the idea of utility or usefulness. Utilitarianism was developed by two Englishmen, Jeremy Bentham (1748–1832) and John Stewart Mills (1806–1873), who were contemporaries of Kant. Bentham and Mills believed that an act is right if it is useful to bring about the best consequences overall. In other words, the best solution would be the one producing the greatest amount of happiness. In essence the "ends justify the means." According to Bentham's philosophy, actions are right to the extent that they promote happiness and pleasure for everyone concerned, and wrong to the degree that they produce pain and no pleasure. Utilitarianism may be divided into two categories: act and rule.

Act Utilitarianism affirms that the correct act is the one that produces the greatest ratio of good to bad. In contemplating a solution to an ethical problem, an act utilitarian will generally question, "what good and bad consequences will result from a certain action in a particular situation"? The act utilitarian will not consider any specific moral rule, only the act or action itself.

Rule Utilitarianism proclaims that we should base our actions on the consequences of the rule or rules under which an act or action falls, and not on the consequences of the act or action itself. The rules may be those presented in religious beliefs, such as the Ten Commandments; those offered by professional codes of ethics or conduct; those set forth by professional groups in the best interest of their clients, such as the American Hospital Association's Patient Bill of Rights; or an arbitrary set of beliefs held by an individual.

Deontology	Teleology
Duty-driven	Goal-drive
Means count	Ends count
Kant	Utilitarianism (Bentham/Mills)

Duties

Imaging professionals who use the normative ethical theories of deontology and teleology may integrate other ethical processes, such as *duties,* which are commitments to act in a professional manner. Our duties may confer a sense of responsibility to our professional practice. Knowing what the duties are will provide us information on what and to whom we are held accountable. For example, the duty of nonmaleficence or "do no harm" is a specific theme in the Hippocratic Oath and has been reviewed as an overriding moral guiding the healthcare professional's conduct toward patients.

Principles of Beneficence and Nonmaleficence

Beneficence and nonmaleficence are both essential parts of medical ethics. *Beneficence* in its simplest form means to *do good* and *nonmaleficence* means to *avoid evil.* Society expects imaging professionals to do good. This *good* should involve: law, custom, relationship, and contract. The law of the land, such as legal situations, will provide the imaging professionals with defined guidelines to do good as society sees it. Our society sees good as caring for the sick or producing quality radiographs. Custom will define good, because customs and mores are considered repeated motifs of society. These motifs or patterns will also provide direction toward the good. Offering your professional skills in producing quality radiographs for diagnosis is an established pattern of society. Relationships with individuals, institutions, and society, involving an interactive process, will provide pathways toward the good. A contract designed as an agreement will indicate what the good may be considered to each individual. A contractual agreement for radiology patients may begin when they agree to enter the hospital, clinic, or doctor's office and undergo a series of diagnostic and/or therapeutic procedures.

The primary beneficiary of an imaging professional's good should be the patient, although, there are often multiple recipients to be considered, such as the physician, the institution, and the community. The practice of beneficence can be related to the risk-benefit consideration made in radiation exposure. Patients should undergo radiographic examinations only when the potential risk of not doing so is malfeasance or doing harm. The imaging professional has a strong obligation to bring about nonmaleficence, which is to ensure that their performance is competent and that appropriate patient safety procedures have been implemented.

Nonmaleficence means to avoid evil and is based on a system of weighting. The good must outweigh the risk of evil. When the imaging professional and the patient must come to a decision concerning an invasive radiographic procedure, the imaging professional must intend to do good for the patient. However, will this good outweigh the risk of evil consequences? For example, in an intravenous pyelogram, the procedure may do a great good by diagnosing kidney function and pathology. However, the risk of evil that must be considered is the possibility that the patient may develop an anaphylactic reaction to the injection of contrast media, which could cause severe side affects and even death. Therefore, the imaging professional, including the radiologist, need to consider these decisions by carefully scrutinizing the physical, mental, and emotional abilities of the patient. The patient must understand the significance of the harm before proceeding with the procedure. It is apparent that to do good and avoid evil are of benefit to the patient. Therefore, the decision is made by weighing the good against the possible evil.

Ethicists consider nonmaleficence and beneficence as different levels of the same norm. There are at least four levels of conduct that would fall along a continuum:

1. Do no harm   Nonmaleficence
2. Prevent harm
3. Remove harm when it is being inflicted
4. Bring about positive good   Beneficence

The thought of not harming, preventing, and removing harm emphasizes one problem that faces all imaging professionals when trying to use principles to do right. Each of these levels sounds good; however, all need further interpretation in order to be applied in a particular circumstance. What is harm? How much should be tolerated?

The duty of beneficence is at the positive end of the continuum. Ethicists will address beneficence as a completely separate principle from nonmaleficence. The reasoning is that we make these kinds of distinctions in our thinking about ethical situations daily. It helps us to think about the difference between not harming and actually helping or benefiting someone else. The imaging professional has a positive duty of beneficence toward the patient when the imaging professional has the capacity to promote the patient's well being.

The Right to Autonomy

The right to autonomy or the right of self-determination is perceived as a freedom right. Changes in healthcare technology have seen the development of more sophisticated equipment and modern interventions that could lead to suffering and prolonged lingering of a terminal patient. The imaging professional who will do everything possible to assist the patient, may find the process will lead to regret rather than being an expression of respect for the sanctity of the patient's life. Therefore, patients have become an active negotiator regarding healthcare decisions affecting them. The patient's right to autonomy has come to be accepted as a legitimate moral claim. Immanuel Kant maintained that the role of self-determination is being in control of making choices that would, in accordance with principles, be valid for everyone. Conversely, John Mills established freedom of action. He indicated that each person should be permitted to act according to his/her own convictions. The two theories, from Kant and Mills, maintain that a patient's input can be rational and that the context of the decision must be favorable to the patient.

The patient may participate in protecting their own good and avoidance of their own harm by securing information about the imaging procedure they will be undergoing. Therefore, the patient, the physician, and the imaging professional are responsible for protecting good and avoiding harm in the imaging process. Because our pluralistic society has so many interpretations of beneficence and nonmaleficence, patient autonomy will continue to be a process of conflicts.

Conflicts may arise between beneficence and nonmaleficence, which will often affect patient autonomy. Conflicts arise from complications of doing good with good intentions that may have negative results. They also arise from the attitude that everyone deserves the best in healthcare.

The issue of what a patient has a right to know becomes important. The American Hospital Association has established the *Patient's Bill of Rights*. The twelve points of the Bill of Rights include statements of: respectful care; right to obtain information, treatment and prognosis in terms the patient can understand, and the right to receive, from the physician, information necessary to give informed consent prior to any procedure or treatment. The informed consent must include the risks, duration of incapacity, alternatives, and the name of the person performing the procedure or treatment. The patient has the right to expect a hospital to make reasonable response to his/her requests for services and continuity of service. The process of informed consent should include what will happen during the procedure and what the consequences might be.

A restriction of patient autonomy may be from improper influences that may restrict the patient's choice. The ill patient is already involved in pressured decisions, concerns for his/her health, future, and family. The imaging professional must be careful not to add any other influences that might truly render a patient, unable by loss of personal freedom, to make decisions concerning his/her care. The imaging department environment may be an unsuitable influence. The intimidating atmosphere may frighten the patient past the point of sound decision making. The imaging professional should make every effort to calm and reassure the patient. However, who is ever free from outside influences and influences from the fear of illness?

Serious barriers to autonomy and informed consent come from the medical community itself, such as the physician, the nurse, and imaging professionals. Because these healthcare providers are educated and experienced, they often believe that they know what is best for the patient. Healthcare providers may become confused and angry when a patient refuses treatment or questions their explanations. The patient will, undoubtedly, sense these negative impressions from the healthcare provider. This may reinforce any distrust he/she may have had previously. An irritated, know-it-all imaging professional can frighten the patient into leaving the examination room before diagnosis. Clear communication between the provider and the patient is quite necessary. It is the imaging professional's obligation to communicate and not merely to spout facts. If the patient does not understand, then the informed consent is not present. Imaging professionals must remember to talk *to* the patient and not *at* the patient.

The imaging professional may get so accustomed to the repetition of giving information to patients that the professional does not truly listen to each patient. An example would be a radiographer who is involved in providing all of the information to the patient, yet sounding like a waiter explaining the "catch of the day" instead of the possible complications of the radiographic procedure or treatment. The patient is usually frightened, and when asked if he/she understands, the patient will nod, but with a head empty of understanding.

The imaging professional may be placed in the center of a conflict between a patient's wish to refuse a procedure, and the physician's order for the procedure or treatment. It is imperative that the imaging professional act as an advocate for the patient. Advocacy may require the imaging professional to act as an intermediary between the patient and physician.

Confidentiality

Patient confidentiality is a requirement of every imaging professional. No information concerning the patient should be divulged to any person without a professional need to know. Information should be shared only with those directly involved in the patient's care. *Confidentiality is keeping secrets.* A secret is knowledge that an imaging professional is obligated to conceal. Obligatory secrets are secrets that emanate from the fact that harm will follow if particular knowledge is disclosed.

The American Hospital Association's Patient's Bill of Rights establishes that *the patient has the right to expect that all communication and records pertaining to his/her care be treated as confidential.* All imaging professionals are obligated to uphold this right. Conversations in public places regarding patients should be avoided. Elevator and cafeteria talk about patients and other healthcare professionals can lead to a civil suit. Imaging professionals should not discuss or release patient information to unauthorized individuals without written consent of the patient. The ethical principles of nonmaleficence, beneficence, and fidelity are involved in patient confidentiality.

The imaging professional should access patient information only when it is necessary to perform their professional duties. The law requires that confidential information regarding the patient be disclosed in the following situations:

1. Civil cases
2. Criminal cases
3. Suspected nonaccidental trauma/child abuse
4. Matters of public health and safety

Liability for Disclosure of Confidential Information

When confidential information is revealed by the hospital or healthcare agency and the patient proves damages, the patient may sue on the theory of defamation or invasion of privacy. Where an imaging professional has disclosed confidential information, the patient may seek relief as indicated previously and report the imaging professional to the appropriate professional agency, such as the American Registry of Radiologic Technologists for censure. The patient may also report the imaging professional to the state licensing agency for a hearing to challenge the imaging professional's right to practice his/her profession.

Although the hospital or healthcare agency, as an entity, does not practice medicine or diagnostic imaging, it can be vicariously liable for the acts of its employees under the doctrine of respondeat superior (let the master respond). This is based on the fact that the employer has the duty to control the employee's performance. Therefore, the hospital/healthcare agency is responsible for the actions of the employee. The employer is obligated to control the employee in protecting the patient's privacy. In order to sue successfully for defamation, libel, and/or slander, it is necessary to show that the confidential information disclosed was both unauthorized and untrue.

More importantly, litigation based on the theory of invasion of privacy is a major concern. Patients are entitled to be free of unwarranted disclosure of personal information. A cause of action could arise from the unauthorized disclosure of medical record information if the information would be of such nature as to offend a person of ordinary sensibilities. A potential area for lawsuit for invasion of privacy is disclosure of unauthorized information to insurance companies. In a 1965 case, *Hammonds v. Aetna Casualty and Surety Company* (243 F. Supp. 793), Aetna Casualty was sued by Hammonds because the insurance company induced a physician to reveal confidential medical information. The Ohio court, ruling in favor of Hammonds, said there was a legal and ethical duty to keep patient information confidential, and the physician breached that duty.

In *Horne v. Patton* (287 Sa. 2nd 8242), a 1973 Alabama case, a doctor revealed medical data to a patient's employer with authorization, resulting in the termination of the job of the patient-employee. The court held that an employer does not necessarily have a legitimate interest in an employee's health history.

The fear of litigation makes custodians of medical records and radiographic film cautious. The release of confidential information is based on:

1. The authorization of the patient
2. A judicial mandate
3. Statutory mandate, such as reporting communicable disease or child abuse

Ethical questions abound in the imaging profession. It is clear that there are no easy answers to many of these questions. Through codes of ethics, the imaging profession has provided a framework to direct, coordinate, and assist the imaging professional practicing in the challenging and constantly changing healthcare delivery system. Imaging professionals must understand codes of ethics, abide by their principles, and respect the individual autonomy and dignity of the patient.

The HIPAA Privacy Rule

The Standards for Privacy of Individually Identifiable Health Information (privacy rule) establishes, for the first time, a set of national standards for the protection of certain health information. The U.S. Department of Health and Human Services (HHS) issued the privacy rule to implement the requirement of the Health Insurance Portability and Accountability Act (HIPAA) of 1996. The privacy rule became effective on April 14, 2001. The privacy rule's standards address the use and disclosure of individuals' health information, referred to as *protected health information* by organizations subject to the privacy rule, referred to as *covered entities*, as well as standards for individuals' rights to understand and control how their health information is used. Within HHS, the Office for Civil Rights (OCR) has responsibility for implementing and enforcing the privacy rule with respect to voluntary compliance activities and civil monetary penalties.

A major goal of the privacy rule is to assure that individuals' health information is properly protected, while allowing the flow of health information needed to provide and promote high-quality healthcare and to protect the public's health and well being. The rule strikes a balance that permits important uses of information, while protecting the privacy of people who seek care and healing. Given that the healthcare marketplace is diverse, the rule is designed to be flexible and comprehensive enough to cover the variety of uses and disclosures that need to be addressed. To view the entire privacy rule and for other additional helpful information about how it applies, access the OCR's Web site: http://www.hhs.gov/ocr/hipaa.

Code of Ethics: American Registry of Radiologic Technologists

This Code of Ethics from the American Registry of Radiologic Technologists (ARRT) is to serve as a guide by which radiologic technologists may evaluate their professional conduct as it relates to patients, colleagues, other members of the allied professions, and healthcare consumers. The Code of Ethics is not law, but is intended to assist radiologic technologists in maintaining a high level of ethical conduct and in providing for the protection, safety, and comfort of patients (American Registry of Radiologic Technologists, ARRT Rules and Regulations: *www.arrt.org/certification/certgenelig.htm*).

Principle 1

The radiologic technologist conducts him/herself in a professional manner, responds to patient needs and supports colleagues and associates in providing quality patient care.

Principle 2

The radiologic technologist acts to advance the principle objective of the profession to provide services to humanity with full respect for the dignity of mankind.

Principle 3

The radiologic technologist delivers patient care and services unrestricted by the concerns of personal attributes or the nature of the disease or illness, and without discrimination regardless of sex, race, creed, religion, or socioeconomic status.

Principle 4

The radiologic technologist practices technology founded upon theoretical knowledge and concepts, utilizes equipment and accessories consistent with the purposes for which they have been designed, and employs procedures and techniques appropriately.

Principle 5

The radiologic technologist assesses situations, exercises care, discretion and judgment, assumes responsibility for professional decisions, and acts in the best interest of the patient.

Principle 6

The radiologic technologist acts as an agent through observation and communication to obtain pertinent information for the physician to aid in the diagnosis and treatment management of the patient, and recognizes that interpretation and diagnosis are outside the scope and practice for the profession.

Principle 7

The radiologic technologist utilizes equipment and accessories, employs techniques and procedures, performs services in accordance with an accepted standard of practice, and demonstrates expertise in minimizing the radiation exposure to the patient, self, and other members of the healthcare team.

Principle 8

The radiologic technologist practices ethical conduct appropriate to the profession, and protects the patient's right to quality radiologic technology care.

Principle 9

The radiologic technologist respects confidences entrusted in the course of professional practice, respects the patient's right to privacy, and reveals confidential information only as required by law or to protect the welfare of the individual or the community.

Principle 10

The radiologic technologist continually strives to improve knowledge and skills by participating in educational and professional activities, sharing knowledge with colleagues, and investigating new and innovative aspects of professional practice. One means available to improve knowledge and skill is through professional continuing education.

Rules of Ethics: American Registry of Radiologic Technologists

The Rules of Ethics is the second part of the *Standards of Ethics*. They are mandatory and directive specific standards of minimally acceptable professional conduct for all presently registered technologists and applicants. Certification is a method of assuring the medical community and the public that an individual is qualified to practice within the profession. Because the public relies on certificates and registrations issued by the ARRT, it is essential that registered technologists and applicants act consistently with these Rules of Ethics. These rules are intended to promote the protection, safety, and comfort of patients. The Rules of Ethics are enforceable. Registered technologists and applicants engaging in any of the following conduct or activities have violated the Rules of Ethics and are subject to the following sanctions:

1. Employing fraud or deceit in procuring or attempting to procure, maintain, renew, or obtain reinstatement of: (1) employment in radiologic technology or a state permit, license, or registration certificate to practice radiologic technology, such as by altering in any respect a certificate of registration with the ARRT; or (2) a certificate of registration with ARRT.
2. Subverting or attempting to subvert ARRT's examination process. Conduct that subverts or attempts to subvert ARRT's examination process includes, but is not limited to:

a. Conduct that violates the security of ARRT examination materials, such as removing examination materials from an examination room, or having unauthorized possessions of any portion of or information concerning a future, current, or previously administered examination of ARRT, or disclosing information concerning any portion of a future, current, or previously administered examination of the ARRT, or disclosing what purports to be, or under all circumstances is likely to be understood by the recipient as, any portion of or "inside" information concerning any portion of a future, current or previously administered examination of the ARRT.

b. Conduct that in any way compromises ordinary standards of test administration, such as communicating with another examinee during administration of the examination, copying another examinee's answers, permitting another examinee to copy one's answers, or possessing unauthorized materials.

c. Impersonating an examinee or permitting an impersonator to take the examination on one's own behalf.

3. Convictions, criminal proceedings, or military court-martials as described below:

a. Conviction of a crime, including a felony, a gross misdemeanor, or a misdemeanor, with the sole exception of speeding and parking violations. All alcohol and/or drug violations must be reported. Offenses that occurred while a juvenile and that are processed through the juvenile system are not required to be reported to the ARRT.

b. Criminal proceedings where a finding or verdict of guilt is made or returned but the adjudication of guilt is either withheld, deferred, or not entered or the sentence is suspended or stayed; or a criminal proceeding where the individual enters a plea of guilty or nolo contendere (no contest).

c. Military court-martials that involve substance abuse, any sex-related infractions, or patient-related infractions.

4. Failure to report to the ARRT that charges regarding the person's permit, license, or registration certificate to practice radiologic technology or any other medical or allied health profession are pending or have been resolved adversely to the individual in any state, territory, or county. Or that the individual has been refused a permit, license, or registration certificate to practice radiologic technology or other allied health profession by another state, territory, or country.

5. Failure or inability to perform radiologic technology with reasonable skill and safety.

6. Engaging in unprofessional conduct, including, but not limited to:

a. A departure from or failure to conform to applicable federal, state, or local government rules regarding radiologic technology practice or, if no such rule exists, to the minimal standards of acceptable and prevailing radiologic technology practice.
b. Any radiologic technology practice that may create unnecessary danger to a patient's life, health, or safety. Actual injury to a patient need not be established under this clause.
c. Any practice that is contrary to the ethical conduct appropriate to the profession that results in the termination from employment. Actual injury to the patient or the public need not be established under this clause.

7. Delegating or accepting the delegation of a radiologic technology function or any other prescribed healthcare function when the delegation or acceptance could reasonably be expected to create an unnecessary danger to a patient's life, health, or safety. Actual injury to a patient need not be established under this clause.
8. Actual or potential inability to practice radiologic technology with reasonable skill and safety to patients by reason of illness, use of alcohol, drugs, chemicals, or any other material, or as a result of any mental or physical condition.
9. Adjudication as mentally incompetent, mentally ill, a chemically dependent person, or a person dangerous to the public by a court of competent jurisdiction.
10. Engaging in any unethical conduct, including, but not limited to, conduct likely to deceive, defraud, or harm the public, or demonstrating a willful or careless disregard for the health, welfare, or safety of a patient. Actual injury need not be established under this clause.
11. Engaging in conduct with a patient that is sexual or may reasonably be interpreted by the patient as sexual, or in any verbal behavior that is seductive or sexually demeaning to a patient, or engaging in sexual exploitation of a patient or former patient. This does not apply to preexisting consensual relationships.
12. Revealing a privileged communication from or relating to a patient, except when otherwise required or permitted by law.
13. Knowingly engaging or assisting any person to engage in or otherwise participating in abusive or fraudulent billing practices, including violations of federal Medicare and Medicaid laws or state medical assistance laws.
14. Improper management of patient records, including failure to maintain adequate patient records or to furnish a patient record of report required by law, or making or causing or permitting anyone to make false, deceptive, or misleading entry in any patient record.
15. Knowingly aiding, assisting, advising, or allowing a person without a current and appropriate state permit, license, or registration certificate or a current certificate of registration with ARRT to engage in the practice of radiologic technology, in a jurisdiction that requires a person to have such a current and

appropriate state permit, license, or registration certificate or a current and appropriate certificate of registration with ARRT in order to practice radiologic technology in such jurisdiction.

16. Violating a rule adopted by any state board with competent jurisdiction, an order of such board, or state or federal law relating to the practice of radiologic technology, or any other medical or allied health professional, or a state or federal narcotics or controlled substance law.

17. Knowingly providing false or misleading information that is directly related to the care of a patient.

18. Practicing outside the scope of practice authorized by the individual's current state permit, license, or registration certificate or the individual's current certificate of registration with the ARRT.

19. Making a false statement or knowingly providing false information to ARRT or failing to cooperate with any investigation of the ARRT or the Ethics Committee.

20. Engaging in false, fraudulent, deceptive, or misleading communications to any person regarding the individual's education, training, credentials, experience, or qualifications, or the status of the individual's state permit, license, or registration certificate in radiologic technology or certificate of registration with the ARRT.

21. Knowing of a violation or a probable violation of any Rule of Ethics by any Registered Technologist or by a Candidate and failing to promptly report in writing the same to the ARRT.

22. Failing to immediately report to his or her supervisor information concerning an error made in connection with imaging, treating, or caring for a patient. For purposes of this rule, errors include any departure from the standard of care that reasonably may be considered to be potentially harmful, unethical, or improper (commission). Errors also include behavior that is negligent or should have occurred in connection with a patient's care, but did not (omission). The duty to report under this rule exists whether or not the patient suffered any injury.

Euthanasia

All hospitals must now have written policies and procedures describing how patient rights are protected at their institutions. Healthcare organizations must establish policies and procedures on euthanasia. In establishing such policies, healthcare providers must take into consideration state and federal law, the opinion of the primary physician, and the patient's wishes, as documented in the patient's medical record.

The Patient Self-Determination Act (1992) requires hospitals and nursing homes to inform incoming patients of their rights concerning the use of life-sustaining treatment. Patients can then choose to develop instructions as to what to do in the event such treatment becomes necessary.

Humanistic Healthcare

The law permits abortion and euthanasia (North Carolina, Ohio, Oregon, Utah, and Wyoming do not have statutes criminalizing assisted suicide (Euthanasia.com Web site: www.euthanasia.com/index.html)). However, this may be in direct conflict with the radiographer's morals or ethics. There are many other instances where the law and ethics are not necessarily compatible. There are also times when the two disciplines are so interrelated that they are indistinguishable. Although similar at times, the two disciplines are not the same and should not be equated so by the radiographer. Changing social definitions of the quality of life should be considered and integrated with clinical care.

The early Greek physicians recognized that sick people often get well if nothing is done to the patient. This is also reflected in the Latin phrase: *vix medicatrix naturae*, which means "to recognize the healing power of nature."

Humanistic healthcare provides an overall understanding of the implications of healthcare. It helps to analyze the various issues involved in ethical decisions and to make humanistic ethical decisions based on appropriate data and information. Finally, it familiarizes the radiographer with his/her responsibilities and accountability for humanistic behavior in providing healthcare to patients.

Comparison between Ethics and Law

Ethics	Law
Internal	*External*
Concerned with motive	Concerned with acts or conduct
Concerned with the interests of the individual and society	Concerned with the interests of society
Right: something to which one has a morally justified claim	Right: power or privilege inherent in a person or enforceable in a court of law

It is impossible to give a right or wrong answer to the ethical vignettes that follow. Therefore, the "answer" to the vignette will be a reaction to the situation in which various sides will be identified and presented. Various questions will be raised, and the writer encourages the reader to look at those questions with an open mind. Perhaps the reader will become aware of aspects of the problem about which he/she was previously ignorant. The purpose of this approach is to stimulate the reader to think of the multifaceted relationship of such complex ethical healthcare problems. The final and ultimate right or wrong answers are the province of the reader.

The reader should raise questions that are not always adequately addressed by the ultimate decision makers. It is hoped the implications of those decisions will be understood in a more profound way.

Vignette 15

Intoxicated Radiologist

Rita Rad, R.T., is a staff radiographer at Spatial Medical Center. Doctor Andrew Angstrom is the resident radiologist for the morning. Rad has noticed that Dr. Angstrom appears to have been drinking when he arrives at the department. Dr. Angstrom seems short-tempered and has a definite odor of alcohol on his breath.

Rita Rad was preparing Barbara Blooming for a scheduled intravenous pyelogram. Dr. Angstrom was called to inject the contrast media into Blooming. After the injection, Dr. Angstrom said, " I'm going over to the cafeteria for a cup of coffee." As soon as he left the x-ray suite, Blooming turned to the radiographer and said, "He smells like a brewery. He's drunk, isn't he? Does he know what he's doing in that condition?"

What, if anything, is the appropriate response in this situation?

What is the ethical issue involved?

What is the radiographer's ethical duty and responsibility to the patient, to Spatial Hospital, and to the radiologist?

Answer

Value components exist in every medical decision. The radiologist has pledged loyalty to the profession, expressed in the traditional Hippocratic Oath and the American Medical Association Code of Ethics. Certain behavior is dictated by the professional organization.

The concern for the patient's competent care is not the issue. The question is, does the patient have a right to a truthful answer? Is the duty to tell the truth unconditional? Could it be argued that an intentional untruth is in the patient's best interest? Or is truth telling an independent act, which is always required regardless of harmful consequences resulting from the truthful disclosure? The fundamental question: Is it morally acceptable to withhold requested information that is potentially meaningful to a patient?

Should the radiographer deceive or mislead the patient when it is believed to be beneficial to the patient? It is an incontrovertible fact of law that all healthcare practitioners have an obligation to protect the patient from being subjected to harmful care. The code of ethics of every healthcare profession dictates a fiduciary duty to the patient also. This involves an accountability, that is, a public trust in providing healthcare services to society that assumes sound judgment be used in giving care competently.

Vignette 16

Experimental Radiotherapy

Mary Mottle was a 68-year-old widow with a diagnosis of malignant melanoma. She was being treated at Quantum Medical Clinic with radiotherapy. The radiotherapy dose was experimental; it has been used in animals, but not as yet in humans. Mottle was given a year to live. She wanted to spend the remaining year with her daughter and grandchildren in another state. When she arrived at her daughter's, they began to look for a hospital or radiotherapy clinic to continue the experimental radiotherapy. No hospital was available for the experimental radiation dose treatments because none were convinced the radiation treatment was clinically sound.

It was suggested that Mottle fly back to Quantum Medical Clinic for continued treatment and let Medicare pay for the expenses. On inquiring about the charges and expenses, she learned that Medicare would not pay for the transportation charges. Therefore, Mottle would not be able to have treatment because she was unable to pay for the flight.

There had been some indication that the radiation treatments were helping Mottle because she was feeling much better.

What, if anything, should be done in this case for the patient or the experimenters of the radiotherapy treatment?

Answer

Mary Mottle's radiotherapy treatment was expensive and controversial. The prolongation of life was in doubt. There are only so many funds available and there are others competing for the same funds.

Would this be considered a medical or sociopsychological need?

Review Questions

1. Which of the following defines morality?
   a. Statute
   b. Fidelity to conscience
   c. The good of society
   d. Manmade rules

2. A radiographer who takes the life of a terminally ill patient would be charged with _____.
   a. Negligence
   b. Personal liability
   c. Murder
   d. Carelessness

3. All of the following are ethical considerations for radiographers except:
   a. Conduct with dignity to the profession
   b. Biased attitude toward race, creed, color, or nature of health problem
   c. Prevent unethical conduct and illegal activities
   d. The right to do no harm

4. Ethical considerations are subject to philosophical, _____, and individual interpretations of what is right or wrong in a particular situation.
   a. Psychological
   b. Legal
   c. Scientific
   d. Theological

5. The American Registry of Radiologic Technologists Code of Ethics serves two major functions: regulation and _____.
   a. Education
   b. Morality
   c. Legality
   d. Autonomy

6. Which of the following has the regulative powers to enforce the ethical codes?
   a. ARRT (American Registry of Radiologic Technologists)
   b. ARRET (American Registry of Radiographic Ethical Technologists)
   c. CRT (Certified Radiologic Technologist)
   d. AMA (American Medical Association)

Chapter 8

Patient's Bill of Rights

Upon completion of Chapter 8, the reader will be able to:

1. Relate the importance of the Patient's Bill of Rights.
2. Interpret the Patient's Bill of Rights published by the American Hospital Association.

Patient's Bill of Rights

It is a somewhat sad commentary on the health profession that a patient bill of rights must be committed to a statement in writing or to legislative enactments. Patient rights should be self-evident. The simple fact is that patients are entitled to dignity, consideration, and self-determination. Many state legislatures have passed a Patient's Bill of Rights document either as a resolution or as statutory law. Some jurisdictions have limited the Patient's Bill of Rights to nursing homes, and others have extended it to include healthcare agencies. California statute states that it requires the Patient's Bill of Rights be posted in all hospitals and medical centers. The healthcare facility exists to serve the patient. The patient does not exist to serve as a hospital commodity or as teaching and research material for the healthcare system. Due to the complexity of the system and some of the reported abuses, it is necessary to inform patients of their rights while undergoing care. The patient should be made aware that he/she has the right to accept or reject treatments recommended by the physician or hospital staff, the right of privacy, the right to be free from unnecessary risk of injury, and the right to determine what is to be done to his/her body.

There is a consensus that the purpose of the patient's bill of rights is to reaffirm the concern of healthcare practitioners for the patient's human dignity. This reaffirmation is a new commitment to quality healthcare for all citizens and marks a new revolution for all healthcare consumers. The U.S. Constitution is a viable document and must be operative in all healthcare facilities for all patients.

A *right* has been defined as a claim to which man is entitled. A *right* by its nature is recognized by law and enforceable in a court of law. The following is the Patient's Bill of Rights published by the American Hospital Association.

1. **Considerate and Respectful Care**: The patient has the right to considerate and respectful care. Radiographers must be polite, display the appropriate respect, and be empathetic to the patient's needs.
2. **Complete and Current Information**: The patient has the right to obtain from his physician complete, current information concerning the diagnosis, treatment, and prognosis in terms the patient can reasonably be expected to understand. When it is not medically advisable to give such information to the patient, the information should be made available to an appropriate person in his behalf. He has the right to know, by name, the physician responsible for coordinating his care. Radiographers must recognize the right of any patient who does not speak English to have access to an interpreter.
3. **Informed Consent**: The patient has the right to receive from his physician information necessary to give informed consent prior to the start of any procedure and/or treatment. Except in emergencies, information for informed consent should include, but not necessarily be limited to, the specific procedure and/or treatment, the medically significant risks involved, and the probable duration of incapacitation. Where medically significant alternatives for care or treatment exist, or when the patient requests information concerning medical alternatives, the patient has the right to such information. The patient also has the right to know the name of persons responsible for the procedures and/or treatment.
4. **Right to Refuse Treatment**: The patient has the right to refuse treatment to the extent permitted by law and to be informed of the medical consequences of his/her action.
5. **Right to Privacy**: The patient has the right to every consideration of his privacy concerning his own medical care program. Case discussion, consultation, examination, and treatment are confidential and should be conducted discreetly. Those not directly involved in his/her care must have the permission of the patient to be present.
6. **Confidentiality** The patient has the right to expect that all communications and records pertaining to his/her care should be treated as confidential.
7. **Reasonable Response to Requests:** The patient has the right to expect that, within its capacity, a hospital must make reasonable response to the request of a patient for services. The hospital must provide evaluation, service, and/or

referral as indicated by the urgency of the case. When medically permissible, a patient may be transferred to another facility only after he/she has received complete information and explanation concerning the need for, and alternatives to, such a transfer. The institution to which the patient is to be transferred must first have accepted the patient for transfer.

8. **Conflict of Interest**: The patient has the right to obtain information as to any relationship of his/her hospital to other healthcare and education institutions insofar as his care is concerned. The patient has the right to obtain information as to the existence of any professional relationships among individuals, by name, who are treating him/her.

9. **Human Experimentation**: The patient has the right to be advised if the hospital proposes to perform human experimentation affecting his/her care or treatment. The patient has the right to refuse to participate in such research projects.

10. **Continuity of Care**: The patient has the right to expect reasonable continuity of care. He has the right to know in advance what appointment times and physicians are available and where. The patient has the right to expect that the hospital will provide a mechanism whereby he/she is informed by his/her physician or a delegate of the physician of the patient's continuing healthcare requirements following discharge.

11. **Explanation of Bill**: The patient has the right to examine and receive an explanation of his/her bill regardless of source of payment.

12. **Hospital Rules and Regulations:** The patient has the right to know what hospital rules and regulations apply to his/her conduct as a patient.

The patient's right to information does not place an obligation on the radiographer to provide any and all information that may be requested. Radiographers must be prepared to offer explanations of the radiographic procedures and to identify themselves and the radiologists. Questions regarding diagnosis, treatment, and other aspects of care must be referred to the patient's physician and/or the radiologist.

Additional contemporary ethical–legal issues dealing with patient's rights are abortion, the right to die, child abuse, involuntary commitment, informed consent, confidentiality, and invasion of privacy. There are other issues, but the above are the most controversial.

Vignette 17

Invasion of Privacy Situation

Opal Opaque was a 45-year-old diabetic patient of many years. She was scheduled for an upper gastrointestinal series at Dynamic View Medical Center. Fanny Phosphor was a radiography student assigned to assist the radiologist with Opaque's radiographic procedure. Phosphor reviewed Opaque's chart and felt she would be an interesting case to present at the weekly student conference and film critique. Phosphor consulted with her instructor, Betty Beam, R.T., who advised Phosphor that Opaque's would be an appropriate case for the conference and film critique on the gastrointestinal system presently being studied.

Phosphor began to talk more with Opaque and learned she had an alcohol problem. Phosphor also learned that Opaque's husband was unfaithful and Opaque knew he had a young lover. Opaque told the student radiographer that she believed these things kept her diabetic condition irregular. At no time did Phosphor reveal to Opaque that she would be the subject of a weekly conference.

Phosphor made an excellent presentation of the patient's case, including the film critique at the conference. She brought out the effect of the alcohol and fidelity problems on Opaque's condition because she believed the staff would have a better understanding of Opaque's radiographic diagnosis. Following the conference, Phosphor was called to the phone and she inadvertently left her notebook with Opaque's case presentation in the conference room. Phosphor became busy with other radiographic procedures and completely forgot about the notes.

The radiology receptionist entered the conference room and found the student's notebook. The receptionist noticed that the notebook had Opaque's name on it and returned it to Opaque's hospital room.

During visiting hours, Opaque's husband happened to see the notebook and noticed that the name and room number on the notes were those of his wife. He read the student's notes regarding his wife's problems. He asked to see the supervising nurse and demanded to know why his wife was used for a radiography conference without her knowledge or permission. He also wanted to know why the slanderous and libelous statements about unfaithfulness were made about him. Opaque's husband told the nursing supervisor that he intended to sue Phosphor, the instructor Betty Beam, everyone present at the radiography conference, and the hospital for invasion of privacy and defamation of character.

What will be the legal outcome?

Should Opal Opaque have been informed of the conference?

Was Opal Opaque's privacy invaded?

Answer

All persons present at the radiography conference are involved in the care of the patient and have a legitimate interest in information relating to the patient. Another issue not easily resolved is whether the communications made to Fanny Phosphor, student radiographer, were confidential and never intended to be exposed to any other persons. If Opal Opaque had known such information would be repeated, she would probably not have disclosed it to Phosphor.

It is obvious that poor judgment was used by the healthcare personnel in this situation. It would not appear that a cause of action for invasion of privacy could be sustained by Opal Opaque because the conference audience was made up of healthcare personnel. Because the radiology receptionist did not read the information, there is no need to address whether she has a "legitimate interest" in the information.

It was Opal Opaque who gave the information about her husband's infidelity to Fanny Phosphor, so the action would appear to be against the wife rather than the radiography student. More importantly, truth is a defense to slander. Opaque's husband would have to prove that the statements were untrue and that he was economically harmed by them.

Vignette 18

Right of Privacy Situation

Emma Insulator, R.T., is a staff radiographer at Cavitation Medical Center and has worked in the radiography department for two years. Recently, a new radiographer, Ronnie Rheostat, R.T., was hired to work the 3 to 11 p.m. shift. Insulator notices that Rheostat talks to all of the patients, asking them a number of questions of a personal nature not related to the radiography procedure.

One day she and Rheostat were assigned to the same lunch period. While on the way to the cafeteria, the two radiographers were on the elevator and Rheostat said that one of the patients, Silvia Sinewave, told her that she had been living with a prominent surgeon who was on staff at Cavitation Medical Center and had an illegitimate child by him. Rheostat continued nonstop relating incidents about Sinewave.

Insulator was concerned about Rheostat's monologue regarding Sinewave. There were other people on the elevator, but Rheostat seemed completely unaware of them.

What, if any, legal implications are involved in this set of circumstances?

Answer

Discussing a patient's case on elevators, in cafeterias, or other public areas is a breach of the fiduciary trust and right to confidentiality to which patients are entitled as part of the "due care" owed by the institution. It can also be an invasion of privacy. This right to privacy was interpreted by the U.S. Supreme Court to exist for every citizen as part of the Constitutional rights and is, therefore, an inherent right. The First Amendment, which provides for freedom of speech and religion, has been interpreted as protecting the citizen's right to privacy.

It is unethical and unprofessional to discuss anything of a private or personal nature concerning the patient. This is one of the most abused areas in patient relations. In the past, there was segregation in most hospitals for hospital employees and visitors, and this physical separation prevented visitors from overhearing employees' conversations. Today, most hospitals share all facilities, and more contact between hospital personnel and visitors result. If hospital personnel are not cognizant of their professional responsibilities not to reveal any information about the patients, they should know that the discussions that take place between the patient and the hospital personnel are considered confidential communications. Any access to the patient's records or other data would come under the same classification.

The patient, as in this case, has the right to be protected from any disclosure of information that would embarrass, stigmatize, or cause her to be held in less esteem. This is not the same as privileged communication.

Privileged communication has special protection under the law. It traditionally has been recognized to exist between an attorney and client, clergyman and church member, or psychiatrist and patient. Where communication is privileged, the confidence entrusted in the course of the professional capacity cannot be revealed and has special immunities.

All professional associations, including the American Society of Radiologic Technologists, are governed by a code of ethics that addresses itself to the issue of not repeating or communicating any information relating to the patient without appropriate or justifiable reasons.

This is obviously a necessary requirement so that patients can feel free to discuss their problems, their illnesses, and other personal matters, in the full assurance that nothing will be repeated. The law considers the unnecessary disclosure of confidential information improper. To discuss the patient's confidential information with a third party is a breach of confidence. It is an unlawful disclosure for which the patient may have a cause of action against the party revealing such information

Review Questions

1. Which of the following rights in the Patient's Bill of Rights will allow a terminally ill patient to refuse treatment, unless the patient is incompetent?
   a. Considerate, respectful care
   b. Right to refuse
   c. Conflict of interest
   d. Confidentiality

2. Which of the following patient rights require disclosing if the hospital or clinical facility is owned by the physician?
   a. Conflict of interest
   b. Right to privacy
   c. Reasonable response to request
   d. Continuity of care

3. Which of the following rights will ensure that the patient understands the statement for payment of hospital services?
   a. Hospital rules and regulations
   b. Continuity of care
   c. Conflict of interest
   d. Explanation of bill

4. Which of the following patient rights will ensure that the patient understands the procedure, risks, and alternatives to the procedure?
   a. Right to refuse treatment
   b. Complete and current information
   c. Informed consent
   d. Considerate and respectful care

5. Which patient's right will allow review of the medical records?
   a. Hospital rules and regulations
   b. Continuity of care
   c. Confidentiality
   d. Complete and current information

6. Which right must provide, to the patient, highly skilled professional care referral for other medical service?
   a. Reasonable response to request
   b. Considerate respectful care
   c. Complete and current information
   d. Continuity of care

7. Which one of the following rights will render a moral obligation by providing the patient his/her diagnosis and treatment in terminology that he/she can understand?
   a. Informed consent
   b. Reasonable response to request
   c. Complete and current information
   d. Confidentiality

Chapter 9

Radiology Service in the Hospital

Upon completion of Chapter 9, the reader will be able to:

1. Appraise the importance of the Joint Commission on the Accreditation of Healthcare Organizations.
2. Identify the list of department policy and procedures manuals.
3. Relate the importance of the radiology request for service form.
4. List the functions of the medical record and/or the radiology report.
5. Identify the medicolegal use of radiographs.
6. Recall the policy of ownership of radiographs established by the American College of Radiology.
7. Relate the importance of retaining radiographic films, using radiographic films as evidence, and marking films for identification.

The Joint Commission on the Accreditation of Healthcare Organizations

The purpose of the Joint Commission on the Accreditation of Healthcare Organizations (JCAHO) is threefold:

1. To establish standards
2. To conduct surveys
3. To award accreditation

The commission serves as an evaluator and educator rather than inspector or judge. It acts as a consultant, helping to identify both strong and weak points, and provides guidelines to assist in correcting the weaknesses. The JCAHO has become a colloquium through which healthcare providers and related human services can be effectively motivated toward higher levels of quality and care.

The JCAHO is not a federal or state regulatory agency. It is a private, nonprofit corporation whose purpose is voluntary accreditation. Accreditation is based on ideal and achievable standards. Standards are developed from a desire to improve the quality of a particular facet of healthcare services. Changes in state-of-the-art medical practices and equipment as well as government regulations precipitate the need to review, revise, and develop new JCAHO standards. Consumer demands for accountability and the rising costs in healthcare have become important concerns in the revision and development of standards.

The standards of the JCAHO recommend the following policies with regards to radiology services:

1. The radiology services in the hospital/medical center are directed by a qualified radiologist who is recognized by the American Board of Radiology.
2. There shall be adequate numbers of technical staff to conduct radiology services.
3. There shall be sufficient space, equipment, and supplies for the performance of radiology services.
4. There shall be written policies and procedures governing radiology services.

Every hospital and/or medical center that is accredited by the JCAHO recommends that the radiologist be an active member of the medical staff, and be available on a full-time or part-time basis, depending on the size and complexity of the radiology services. The radiology department director and/or administrative technologist should establish an effective working relationship with the medical staff, the hospital administrator, and other department services. The radiologist shall provide authenticated reports of radiologic findings. A radiation physicist should be available as needed for consultation, radiation safety, and education purposes.

Policies and Procedures

It is the responsibility of the radiology department administrator to develop and approve all radiology department policies and procedures. When this responsibility is executed thoroughly, the radiology department should function in a smooth and organized manner. The following list of department policy manuals should be available in every radiology department:

1. Department policy and procedure manual
2. Quality assessment and improvement manual
3. Infection control manual

4. Safety manual
5. Hazardous waste policy and procedures
6. Emergency preparedness manual/disaster plan
7. Continuing education manual
8. Administrative manual
9. Human Resources policies and procedures
10. Job descriptions, purpose, mission, and organizational charts

Requesting Radiologic Services

Requests for radiographic examinations are referred to the department of radiology. The radiologist reviews each request prior to the examination. Completeness of information pertinent to the patient's condition is important. Patient preparation, infection control, isolation information, and detailed instructions on how to move or transport the patient should be indicated on the request form. It is the responsibility of the radiology department manager and the radiologist to see that these examinations are performed promptly and efficiently according to the radiation safety criteria and legal codes.

Procedures Manual

Procedures manuals are designed to meet joint accreditation standards, state standards, and hospital codes. The procedures manual should cover subjects such as appropriate gowning of the patient; transportation of the patient; precautions to be observed in the transportation of the very confused, ill-medicated, or feeble patient; and patient isolation. In addition, sequencing of each radiographic procedure using contrast media is included in the manual. The description of each radiographic examination covered in the manual includes the details of the procedure, as well as the preparation for the study.

Vignette 19

Review Patient History

It is the responsibility of the radiologist to review the medical records of all in-house patients prior to any diagnostic examination. The radiologist, Dr. Watt, and the radiologic technologist, Amy Ohms, were performing an upper gastrointestinal series on Sally Syncope. Dr. Watt instructed the patient to step up onto the footboard of the x-ray table to begin the fluoroscopic part of the procedure. Both Dr. Watt and Amy Ohms failed to read the patient's chart, which stated that Syncope had fainting spells prior to being transported to the radiology department. The patient, upon stepping up onto the footboard, fainted and fell to the floor. She sustained a hip fracture that required surgical correction. This unnecessary surgery aggravated a preexisting vascular disorder causing Syncope to develop pulmonary emboli. Who is legally liable for damages and why?

Answer

The radiologist, Dr. Watt, is liable for not being acquainted with the patient, Sally Syncope's, medical history. The hospital is also held liable for failure of the nursing staff to complete the x-ray request form to include the patient's medical condition prior to transportation to the radiology department. In addition, the radiographer, Amy Ohms, was negligent for failure to anticipate the possibility of the patient fainting during the examination. The possibility of any patient fainting during any type of radiographic examination is part of the radiographer's training, and this knowledge imposes a duty to the radiographer to guard against this event or any other harm a patient may endure.

Radiology Reports/Medical Records

The medical records of a patient are a written account of what has happened to the patient during a period of time. This event can occur in a doctor's office, hospital, nursing home, health maintenance organization, or any place in which medical care is given. The medical records and/or the radiologic reports serve many functions:

1. They are a source of accurate communication between health professionals and other legitimate or appropriate persons or agencies.
2. They are official confidential documents, and are the physical property of the hospital or doctor's office or agency.
3. They serve as a database for planning individual care and clinical data.

4. They serve as an objective witness to certain events that occurred in a health-care setting.

The medical records and/or radiology reports are required to contain sufficient information to justify diagnosis, course of illness, management, and treatment. Radiology reports are exclusively diagnostic reports of radiographic examinations.

Many court cases have been won or lost on the information written in the medical record and/or radiographic report. If a person initiates care or performs a procedure on the basis of standing orders or routine, the person doing the procedure should be certain to identify the reasons for the decisions to implement a specific treatment. Radiology reports are written like an investigative report, presenting only facts and not conclusions. Legally, the medical record and/or radiology request or report are important in any malpractice suit; they can be subpoenaed and brought into court. It is essential that the patient's name be correctly spelled. An incorrect name could infer that improper attention was given to the patient. Correct patient identification is basic to conveying accurate information. The method of admission into the hospital and/or the radiology department is important (i.e., stretcher, wheelchair, or ambulance), the time the patient was sent to the radiology department, and the time the patient was released from the radiology department. All pertinent clinical information must be written on the radiology request form.

Medicolegal Use of Radiographs

The radiologist is a consultant to the medical staff giving them reports of diagnostic radiologic examinations and/or treatments. The radiologist must sign the radiologic reports, which then become an integral part of the patient's medical record.

Ownership of Radiographs

Radiographs from private x-ray labs are frequently given to patients who deliver the radiographs to their attending physician. The patient retains ownership. Portable x-ray services also work in this manner. Dental radiographs made by the dentist are part of the dental record. In a private physician's office, the radiographs are the property of the physician and part of the medical record. Radiographs taken in a hospital, clinic, or emergency center are the property of the facility. The patients and their physicians are entitled to the report, but not the radiographs.

Policy of Ownership

The American College of Radiology has adopted the following statement regarding ownership of radiographs for the guidance of hospitals and physicians.

1. Radiographs should be used for the best interest of the patient.
2. Radiographs are the legal property of the radiologist, physician, or hospital in which they were made.
3. It should be the policy of the radiologist to make the radiographs available to the attending physicians with a copy of the report.
4. If the referring physician or the patient, on behalf of the referring physician, wishes to take the films away from the office or hospital, it should be clearly understood that the films are "on loan" and must be returned.
5. If the patient dismisses the referring physician and goes to another physician, the radiographs and reports should be made available to the new physician.
6. If the referring physician, on being dismissed by the patient, objects to the radiographs being sent to the second physician, the radiologist/physician must send the radiographs/reports in spite of the objection.
7. All films should be diagnostic and permanently marked, identified, and dated.
8. When a medicolegal situation exists, the radiologist has the right to refuse to release the radiographs for his own protection, except when the radiographs/reports are subpoenaed by the court.

Retention of Radiographic Films

Radiographic films are utilized for statistical purposes, for illustration of scientific literature, for teaching, and for medicolegal use. Radiographic films should be filed in the department and, after one year, placed in storage vaults that are available for reference. Radiographic film should be kept for a minimum of seven years or until a minor reaches adult age, plus one to three years. For example, in any particular state, if the age of majority is 18 and the statute of limitations for any tort action is 3 years, then the minor would have until 21 years of age to sue.

Radiographic Films Used as Evidence

Radiographic films can be introduced in a court of law as evidence. They can be introduced by the physician who directed the taking of the radiographs, or the radiographer who took the films may be present to identify them.

Marking Films for Identification

Radiographic films are valueless as legal evidence unless there is competent proof of their identity. The patient's name and x-ray number, date, and place must be imprinted on the radiographic film. Right and left markers must be permanently developed on the radiograph.

Radiologists Liable for Errors

A Missouri Appellate Court ruled that two radiologists were liable to a patient for $50,000 in actual damages and $100,000 in punitive damages. The radiological group, which was a general partnership consisting of two radiologists, first x-rayed the patient in 1965 in connection with abdominal complaints. Thirty-two months later, the patient was referred to the same radiological group for x-rays in connection with a complaint of soreness in his ribs. A resident employed by the group reported a lytic lesion in the anterior end of the eleventh rib. The report, which was signed by one of the partners, suggested that the lesion was a malignant tumor that had spread from its original location.

The patient's family physician, who had referred the patient to the radiological group, decided that the rib lesion should be removed for biopsy. A thoracic surgeon performed the operation, but a pathologist found no lesion. Further radiographs disclosed that the lesion was in the tenth rib not the eleventh. A second operation was performed and the lesion was diagnosed as a benign nonmalignant tumor. Testimony showed that the lesion appeared on the 1965 radiographs and was unchanged in the 1967 radiographs.

In the patient's suit against the two radiologists, a jury returned a verdict for the patient for $50,000 in actual damages and $150,000 in punitive damages. The trial court then ordered a remittitur of $50,000 from the award of punitive damages, which the patient accepted under protest. The patient had also sued the resident, but later dismissed him from the case.

On appeal by the physicians, the appellate court said that the question of negligence in failing to look at the 1965 radiographs in the patient's files, and in incorrectly identifying the rib, was properly submitted to the jury.

"It is apparent from the fact that plaintiff's lawyer discovered the earlier lesion in examining the radiographs at the first trial that the discovery of the lesion required no extraordinary medical skill," the court said.

There was testimony by the surgeon that he would not have operated if he had known that the lesion had not grown in 32 months. The surgeon was also sued by the patient, but he settled during the trial.

The court concluded that evidence that the patient had undergone two unnecessary operations supported the submission to the jury of the punitive damages claim (*Smith v. Courter*, 575 SW Second 199, Missouri Court of Appeals, May 1, 1978, rehearing denied, June 12, 1978; transfer denied, January 29, 1978; in *The Citation*, 33(3): 26).

Vignette 20

Department Policy Situation: Employee Relations

The work schedules are posted at least two months in advance. One particular evening, a staff radiographer was scheduled to work 3 to 11 p.m. He did not come to work, nor did he call. This had happened once before. The following evening, he comes to work when he is scheduled to be off. As the supervising radiographer, you ask the radiographer where he was the previous evening. He says that he forgot that he was supposed to work and came to work this evening to make up the time.

What, if any, are some legal risks involved?

Answer

The hospital/medical center has a duty to each and every patient admitted for care to its premises; it has an obligation to implement standards to assure quality care will be maintained. Implicit in this obligation is the right to develop and maintain policies, procedures, rules, and regulations, which give information and guidance to employees who work in the institution.

However, the employee has certain rights. They have the right to know the policy of the hospital and what is expected of them as an employee. They also have the right to know what, if anything, will happen if they fail to meet those expectations set out in the job description or in the policies and procedures of the hospital.

An employee who consistently fails to appear for work without notifying his/her superiors or giving an explanation for his/her unacceptable behavior, is subject to disciplinary actions. The disciplinary actions should be according to the policy of the hospital. Any procedural steps should be according to the policy of the hospital. The supervising radiographer should use clear and concise language in documenting what has taken place. The conference or discussion with the employee should be included in the memorandum. If a future course of action has been decided between the supervising radiographer and the staff radiographer, that also should be included.

The employee should have the opportunity to read the memorandum made by the supervising radiographer and sign it, or the employee should receive a copy of the memorandum, or both, depending on the hospital procedure.

The memorandum should state facts and what the supervising radiographer perceived through his/her sense to be a fact. Judgmental terms and conclusions should be scrupulously avoided. If the staff radiographer refuses to sign the document, this should be noted. A copy of the document should be sent to the appropriate administrative parties, including the Human Resource director.

Review Exercises

1. If a person is found guilty in a criminal case, that person ____.
   a. Will automatically forfeit his license
   b. Will be expected to pay assessed money damages
   c. Will be expected to pay a fine or serve a jail term
   d. Will be acquitted

2. Which of the following will allow for restraints to be applied to a patient against his/her will?
   a. By a nurse's order
   b. When a patient is injurious to himself of other patients
   c. When there is a shortage of medical staff
   d. When the family has requested it

3. The purpose of the Joint Review Commission on the Accreditation of Healthcare organizations is to establish standards, conduct surveys, and to ____.
   a. Punish for infractions
   b. Collect fees
   c. Award accreditation
   d. Regulate

4. Medical records and charts are important and necessary documents for which of the following:
   a. Communication between healthcare radiographers and hospital administrators
   b. Legal evidence as documentation of certain patient events
   c. Research and statistical information for various government agencies
   d. Medical audits and accreditation and licensing processes

5. Medical records and charting should be _____.
   a. Specific, concise, accurate, relevant
   b. Factual rather than opinionated
   c. Source-oriented rather than problem-oriented
   d. Recognized as diminishing in value in the age of computers

6. A medical records document should have a legal signature and _____.
   a. Name only
   b. Name plus professional status
   c. Sufficient data to assure specific identification
   d. Variations according to shift and agency policy

7. Objectivity in documentation, in the medical record, is most easily attained by recording _____.
   a. The facts as you perceive them through your senses
   b. What your co-workers state about the situation
   c. What the patient says about his/her condition
   d. What assumptions you make because of your past experience with the patient

8. An incident report should be _____.
   a. Completed by the radiographer in charge of the area
   b. Completed promptly and only with factual information
   c. Completed with the minimum amount of information
   d. Completed only after contacting the supervisor in charge of the area for guidance

Chapter 10

Licensure, Certification, and Credentialing

Upon completion of Chapter 10, the reader will be able to:

1. Define regulation, certification, licensure, and accreditation.
2. Identify the purpose of licensure.
3. Discuss the concerns of limited licensure.
4. Explain the purpose of certification and accreditation.

Credentialing

In 1981, the U.S. Congress passed into law the Consumer–Patient Radiation Health and Safety Act, Subtitle 1 of Public Law 97-35. The act mandates the Secretary of Health and Human Services to develop federal standards for:

1. The accreditation of educational programs that train radiologic personnel
2. The credentialing of persons who perform radiologic procedures

The standards were issued, and in 1985 were published in the U.S. Department of Health and Human Services' section of the *Federal Register* entitled, "Standards for the Accreditation of Educational Programs for the Credentialing of Radiologic Personnel." These standards were implemented in 50 states, as well as the District of Columbia, Puerto Rico, the Northern Mariana Islands, the Virgin Islands, Guam, American Samoa, and the Trust Territory of the Pacific Islands.

The federal standards were developed as a model to provide a basis for consistency among the states, and are intended to encourage the states to adopt uniform accreditation and credentialing qualifications for radiologic personnel. The federal law will preserve the state's traditional role in the regulation of health professionals. Therefore, compliance with these standards is voluntary; there are no penalties to the states if the standards are ignored. However, one section of the Act established that in the absence of state compliance within three years, the Secretary of Health and Human Services shall report to the Congress recommendations for legislative changes considered necessary to assure the state's compliance with this subtitle. Therefore, these standards were developed as a model for the states in educational accreditation and personnel credentialing. Monitoring the states' conformance with the Act is also mandated.

In 1997, The American Society of Radiologic Technologists (ASRT), a national professional society of more than 104,000 members, launched an aggressive campaign to protect patients from overexposure to radiation during radiologic procedures and help reduce the cost of administering healthcare. During the 1999–2000 and 2001–2002 congressional sessions, the ASRT introduced House and Senate bills that pursue basic education and certification standards for healthcare workers who administer radiologic procedures in all 50 states. The bill, known as the Consumer Assurance of Radiologic Excellence (CARE) bill, would ensure that patients undergoing all types of radiologic procedures have the same assurance of quality as those receiving mammograms under the provisions of the Mammography Quality Standards Act, which was passed by the Congress in 1992.

According to the ASRT position statement, ensuring a minimum level of education, knowledge, and skill for radiologic personnel, the CARE bill or the federal minimum standards will:

1, Ensure that quality information is presented for diagnosis and that quality radiation therapy treatments are delivered, leading to accurate diagnosis, treatment, and cure. Poor quality images can lead to additional testing, delays in treatment, and needless anxiety for the patient.

2. Reduce healthcare costs by lowering the number of radiologic examinations that must be repeated due to improper positioning or poor technique. Repeated radiologic examinations cost the U.S. healthcare system millions of dollars annually in needless medical bills.

3. Improve the safety of radiologic procedures. Administered properly, radiation is an invaluable tool in the diagnosis, treatment, and management of disease. But most radiologic procedures also carry a potential health risk, and radiation can be harmful if incorrectly administered.

The CARE bill is posted on the ASRT Web site:
http://www.asrt.org/media/pdf/care_bill.pdf

The two major credentialing processes in radiography are certification and licensure. Definitions of credentialing terminology, identified as either governmental or nongovernmental including the methods of implementation, are

1. **Regulation:** The intervention of government to control or change the behavior of participants in the marketplace through specifications of rules for the participants.
2. **Licensure:** The process whereby an agency of government grants permission to an individual to engage in a given occupation upon finding that the applicant has met predetermined qualifications and has attained the minimal degree of competence necessary to ensure that public health, safety, and welfare will be reasonably well protected. Licensure of health professionals is controlled by the state governments. Many professionals are licensed in some states, but not in others. Licensure statutes throughout the states will vary considerably.
3. **Certification:** The process by which a nongovernmental agency or organization grants recognition of competence to an individual who has met certain predetermined qualifications specified by that agency or organization. Certification is normally granted by national professional organizations. Certifying organizations customarily dictate education, training, and competency requirements for applicants and offer certificate holders the right to use special professional title designations.
4. **Accreditation**: The process whereby a nongovernmental agency or organization evaluates and recognizes an institution or specialized program of study that meets certain established qualifications and educational standards, through periodic evaluation.
5. **Credentialing:** The recognition of professional or technical competence by the government, private professional groups, and certifying organizations.

Licensure

Licensure is a process by which a government agency authorizes an individual to engage in a given occupation and use a specific title. The professional privileges are contingent on the individual meeting specific predetermined qualifications. Assuring that, at least, a minimum degree of competence has been attained. Licensure is under the control of the state government. Licensure will not guarantee excellence. However, it will ensure, at least, a basic competency level in clinical practice.

States that do not license and regulate radiologic personnel do not require certification of operators of ionizing radiation. Therefore, there are x-ray operators who have less than adequate or no formal training or education in radiologic science. In many states, it is perfectly lawful for a secretary, receptionist, or medical assistant, none of whom have had any formal education in the use of x-rays, including patient and operator safety, to administer ionizing radiation.

The basic purpose of licensure is to try to decrease the harmful effects of excessive and unnecessary amounts of radiation to which the public is being exposed by untrained and incompetent operators of x-ray equipment. The harmful effects of diagnostic radiation do not affect an individual acutely or within years, but in generations, decades, and even centuries later. The harmful effects of radiation on hereditary genes are cumulative and irreversible as they are passed down from generation to generation. Although, individual incidents of radiation-induced deformities or illness are not predictable, what is predictable is that there will be a statistical increase in the incidence of certain deleterious conditions related to an increase in the overall radiation exposure to the population.

Certification

The American Registry of Radiologic Technologists (ARRT) establishes qualifications for certification and for registration in the various disciplines comprising the profession of radiologic technology. Radiologic technology includes, but is not limited to, the disciplines of:

Radiography (R)
Nuclear Medicine Technology (N)
Radiation Therapy (T)
Cardiovascular-interventional Radiography (CV)
Mammography (M)
Computed Tomography (CT)
Magnetic Resonance Imaging (MR)
Quality Management (QM)
Sonography (S)
Bone Densitometry (BD)
Vascular Sonography (VS)
Cardiac-Interventional Radiography (CI)
Vascular-Interventional Radiography (VI)
Breast Sonography (BS)
Radiologist Assistants (RA)

The ARRT evaluates candidates for certification and for registration using the qualifications that it has established, and certifies and registers individuals meeting these qualifications. An important distinction exists between the term *certification* and the term *registration* as used by the ARRT. Individuals having satisfied the requirements for certification described in the ARRT Rules and Regulations are awarded a certificate attesting to the fact that the requirements were met and are, therefore, certified by the ARRT. The individual is registered with the ARRT as a person having met both the requirements for initial certification and the requirements for continued registration as described by the ARRT Rules and Regulations. Notwithstanding a candidate being awarded certification upon the satisfaction of all requirements, certification and/or registration may be revoked as described in Section 9.03 of ARRT Rules and Regulations.

In accordance with ARRT's "Equation for Excellence," candidates for ARRT certification must meet basic requirements in the three components of the equation:

1. **Ethics**: A candidate for certification must be a person of good moral character and must not have engaged in conduct that is inconsistent with the ARRT Standards of Ethics or the Rules and Regulations. The person must agree to comply with the ARRT Rules and Regulations and Standards of Ethics.
2. **Education**: Candidates for certification must have successfully completed a formal educational program accredited by a mechanism acceptable to the ARRT.
3. **Examination**: Candidates, after meeting all other qualifications, must pass an examination developed and administered by the ARRT. The examination will assess the knowledge and cognitive skills underlying the intelligent performance of the tasks typically required by the staff technologist practicing within the respective disciplines.

The ARRT Rules and Regulations and Standards of Ethics are listed on the ARRT Web site: *http://www.arrt.org/certification/certgenelig.html*

Vignette 21

References

Penny Parallax, administrator of radiology services at Mottle Regional Medical Center, has been requested to send references on radiography personnel as part of her overall job function. Recently, Parallax was asked to send information about Nancy Neutron, R.T., an evening staff radiographer. There was a substantial amount of negative information on Neutron in her file. Parallax had several interviews and counseling sessions with Neutron over her five year employment at Mottle Regional Medical Center.

Nancy Neutron, R.T., had been suspended from the medical center for irresponsible behavior including coming on duty intoxicated. If she had continued to work for Mottle Regional Medical Center, it seems inevitable that she would have been asked to resign or would have been fired for incompetence.

Penny Parallax wants to do the honest and right thing in giving a reference. She wants to be fair to Neutron, and she wants to be fair to the potential employer. More specifically, Parallax fears that she may be the subject of a lawsuit for defamation of character if Neutron were to find out that negative information was given and the substance of that information.

What, if any, legal risk is involved for a radiology administrator or supervisor?

Answer

Qualified privilege is a recognized privilege in which the public interest in activities that presupposes frank communication on certain matters between persons who stand in particular relationships to each other outweighs the damage to individuals of good faith, but where defamatory statements are relevant to the interests of those employers involved. This means that when an employer or valid representative of the agency gives an employee an evaluation or reference, that report is considered to be privileged information. The essence of the issue before us is "fair comment." As long as an employer makes his/her observations and comments in a professional manner, without malice or vindictiveness, there is not cause for action for defamation of character.

It is necessary in the workplace for references to be exchanged among employers. The references must be honest and objective. The persons giving the references should be factual and not characterize the employee's acts. This is sometimes difficult to do; however, one should try to refrain from drawing inferences or conclusions. Let the reader of the evaluation do that. There are times when opinions are asked and must be given. The opinions that are given should have a basis in fact. There is no need to fear being sued for defamation of character if one sticks to these simple guidelines or rules.

Review Questions

1. The Consumer–Patient Radiation Health and Safety Act of 1981 was developed as a model to provide consistency among the states to adopt _____ qualifications for radiology personnel.
   a. Licensure
   b. Certification
   c. Registration
   d. Credentialing

2. The two major credentialing processes, in radiography, are certification and _____.
   a. Licensure
   b. Registration
   c. Credentialing
   d. Accreditation

3. The intervention of government to control or change the behavior of participants in the marketplace is called _____.
   a. Licensure
   b. Registration
   c. Credentialing
   d. Accreditation

4. The process by which a nongovernmental agency recognizes the competency of an individual is called _____.
   a. Licensure
   b. Regulation
   c. Certification
   d. Accreditation

5. A nongovernmental agency evaluates and recognizes an institute or special program of study. This is called _____.
   a. Licensure
   b. Registration
   c. Certification
   d. Accreditation

Chapter 11

Medicolegal Concerns for Teleradiology

Upon completion of Chapter 11, the reader will be able to:

1. Define the American College of Radiology standards for teleradiology.
2. Understand the ACR goals for teleradiology.
3. Identify the qualifications of personnel and equipment specifications for teleradiology.
4. Describe licensing, credentialing, and liability, to include quality control, improvement safety, infection control, and patient education concerns.
5. Define the legal issues regarding liability, responsibility, accountability, and duty of care.
6. Understand the security and confidentiality of teleradiologic images.

Introduction to Teleradiology Advances

Technological advances in teleradiology cannot be considered independently of the revolutionary developments that have occurred in the past 20 years in the field of medical imaging, paving the way for the increasingly important role of information technology and telecommunications in healthcare. The diagnostic imaging department of the future will make extensive use of computer networks, mass storage devices, and sophisticated workstations at which humans and machines will interact, assisted by advanced information processing tools and techniques of knowledge engineering, to achieve integration of multimodality imaging data and expert medical knowledge.

Picture archiving and communications systems (PACS) form the core of such an environment, and include the acquisition, storage, communication, display, and manipulation of diagnostic images and related patient data. Teleradiology services build upon and extend this environment to interhospital or hospital-to-point-of-need communications on a regional, national, or global scale. Therefore, teleradiology can be considered as an extended virtual radiology department that encompasses available physical and human resources over a wide region in order to support remote diagnostic procedures and patient management. Possible teleradiology scenarios at various geographical scales include:

1. *Local area services that are within the same building or adjacent buildings of the same hospital* — Radiologist reviews images and provides primary reporting and real-time remote consultation for critical cases, such as patients in the intensive care unit, the emergency department, or the operating room. This effectively corresponds to teleradiology services offered using the resources of a local PACS.
2. *Metropolitan area services that are within the same metropolitan area* — Imaging specialists in a major hospital offer consultation and provide support for specific diagnostic procedures to other hospitals and private physicians in the same metropolitan area.
3. *Wide area or global services that cover an extended geographical region and may cross country borders* — Diagnostic imaging examinations are performed by primary care or rural physicians and can be monitored by specialists at a major referral medical center, who can also provide consultation on the diagnostic interpretation of acquired images. Radiologists in a hospital can consult with colleagues or subspecialists located in other hospitals. Medical imaging specialists in a hospital may also provide support to mobile diagnostic imaging units or units at remote and isolated sites, which may or may not have a radiologist on site.

Teleradiology Services Involve Multimedia Communications

In teleradiology, the basic component of the communication object is the diagnostic image. Additional medical and demographic patient data, the referring physician's comments, and the radiologists' report are of a textual type. Teleconsultation may also involve the real-time transmission of voice and video data. Video frames, from image sequences of dynamic diagnostic imaging procedures and patient monitoring sessions, may also be included as part of the communication object. Current advances in the indexing and management of multimedia data are likely to impact future developments in teleradiology services and applications.

Teleradiology services involve the use of heterogeneous hardware and software systems. The degree to which such systems can be fully integrated will have a significant effect on the efficiency with which such services are provided and, consequently, on their effectiveness and acceptance by the healthcare community. Therefore, integration mechanisms based on a unified user interface, a unified computerized patient record, which may consist of geographically distributed segments, and intelligent distributed hierarchical storage management are absolutely important in any attempt at providing efficient teleradiology services in an integrated healthcare environment (Excerpts from Orphanoudakis et al., 1996. Technological advances in teleradiology, *European Journal of Radiology*, 22: 205–217).

American College of Radiology (ACR) Standard for Teleradiology

The standards of the American College of Radiology (ACR) are not rules, but are guidelines that attempt to define principles of practice that should generally produce high quality radiologic care. The physician and medical physicist may modify an existing standard as determined for the individual patient and by available sources. Adherence to ACR standards will not assure a successful outcome in every situation. The standards should not be deemed inclusive of all proper methods of care, or exclusive of other methods of care reasonably directed to obtaining the same results. The standards are not intended to establish a legal standard of care or conduct, and deviation from a standard does not, in and of itself, indicate or imply that such medical practice is below an acceptable level of care. The ultimate judgment regarding the propriety of any specific procedure or course of conduct must be made by the physician and medical physicist in light of all circumstances presented by the individual situation.

Definition

Teleradiology is the electronic transmission of radiologic images from one location to another for the purpose of interpretation and/or consultation. Teleradiology may allow more timely interpretation of radiologic images and give greater access to secondary consultations and improved continuing education. Users in different locations may simultaneously view images. Appropriately utilized, teleradiology may improve access to radiologic interpretations and, thus, improve patient care.

Teleradiology is not appropriate if the available teleradiology system does not provide images of sufficient quality to perform the indicated task. When a teleradiology system is used to render the official interpretation, there should not be a clinically significant loss of data from image acquisition through transmission to final image display. For transmission of images for display use only, the image quality should be sufficient to satisfy the needs of the clinical circumstance. While not all inclusive, the standard should serve as a model for all physicians and healthcare workers who utilize teleradiology.

Goals

Teleradiology is an evolving technology. New goals will continue to emerge. The current goals of teleradiology include:

- Providing consultative and interpretive radiologic services
- Making radiologic consultations available to medical facilities without onsite radiologic support
- Providing timely availability of radiologic images and image interpretation in emergent and nonemergent clinical care areas
- Facilitating radiologic interpretations in on-call situations
- Providing subspecialty radiologic support as needed
- Enhancing educational opportunities for practicing radiologists
- Promoting efficiency and quality improvements
- Providing interpreted images to referring providers
- Supporting telemedicine
- Providing supervision of offsite imaging studies

Qualifications of Personnel

The radiologic examination at the transmitting site must be performed by qualified personnel trained in the examination to be performed. In all cases, this means a licensed and/or registered radiologic technologist, radiation therapist, nuclear medicine technologist, or sonographer. This technologist must be under the supervision of a qualified licensed physician.

It is desirable to have a qualified medical physicist and/or image management specialist on site or serving as consultants. The following will identify the qualifications of all the personnel involved in teleradiologic services:

1. Physician — The official interpretation of images must be done by a physician who has:
    1. An understanding of the basic technology of teleradiology, its strengths and weaknesses, as well as limitations, and who is knowledgeable in the use of teleradiology equipment.
    2. Demonstrated qualifications as delineated in the appropriate ACR standard for the particular diagnostic modality being transmitted through teleradiology.

2. Radiologic technologist, radiation therapist, nuclear medicine technologist, or sonographer should be:
    1. Certified by the appropriate registry and/or possess unrestricted state licensure.
    2. Trained to properly operate and supervise the teleradiology system.

3. Qualified Medical Physicist — An individual who is competent to practice independently in one or more of the subfields in medical physics. The ACR considers that certification and continuing education in the appropriate subfield(s) demonstrates that an individual is competent to practice one or more of the subfields in medical physics and to be a qualified medical physicist. The ACR recommends that the individual be certified in the appropriate subfield(s) by the American Board of Radiology (ABR).

    The appropriate subfields of medical physics include therapeutic radiologic physics, diagnostic radiologic physics, medical nuclear physics, and radiologic physics.

    Continuing education of a qualified medical physicist should be in accordance with the ACR Standard for Continuing Medical Education (Res. 17, 1996).

4. Image Management Specialist:
    1. The image management specialist is an individual who is qualified to assess and provide problem-solving input, initiate repair, and coordinate system-wide maintenance programs to assure sustainable high-image quality and system function. This individual would also be directly involved with any system expansion programs.
    2. This specialist should be available in a timely manner in case of malfunction to facilitate the return to optimal system functionality.

Equipment Specifications

Specifications for equipment used in teleradiology will vary depending on the individual facility's needs, but in all cases should provide image quality and availability appropriate to the clinical need. Compliance with the ACR/NEMA (National Electrical Manufacturers Association) Digital Imaging and Communication in Medicine (DICOM) Standard is strongly recommended for all new equipment acquisitions, and consideration of periodic upgrades incorporating the expanding features of that standard should be part of the continuing quality-improvement program.

Equipment guidelines cover two basic categories of teleradiology when used for rendering the official interpretation:

1. Small matrix size, such as CT, MRI, sonography, nuclear medicine, digital fluoroscopy, and digital angiography
2. Large matrix size, such as digital radiography and digitized radiographic films

When using small matrix size, the dataset should provide a minimum of a 512 × 512 matrix size at a minimum of an 8-bit pixel depth for processing or manipulation, with no loss of matrix size or bit depth at display. With the large matrix size, the data should allow for a minimum of 2.5 line pair/millimeter (lp/mm) spatial resolution at a minimum of 10-bit pixel depth.

Acquisition or Digitization

Initial image acquisition should be performed in accordance with the appropriate ACR modality or examination standard.

1. Direct Image Capture
   The entire image data set produced by the digital modality both in terms of image matrix size and pixel bit depth should be transferred to the teleradiology system. It is recommended that the DICOM standard be used.

2. Secondary Image Capture
   1. *Small matrix images* — Each individual image should be digitized to a matrix size as large as or larger than that of the original image by the imaging modality. The images should be digitized to a minimum of 8 bits pixel depth. Film digitization or video frame grab systems conforming to the above specifications are acceptable.
   2. *Large matrix images* — These images should be digitized to a matrix size corresponding to 2.5 lp/mm or greater, measured in the original detector plane. The images should be digitized to a minimum of 10 bits pixel depth.

3. General Provisions
   At the time of acquisition, small or large matrix, the system must include annotating *capabilities* including patient name, identification number, date and time of examination, name of facility or institution of acquisition, type of examination, patient or anatomic part orientation, and amount and method of data compression. The capability to record a brief patient history is desirable.

Compression

Data compression may be used to increase transmission speed and reduce storage requirements. Several methods, including both reversible and irreversible techniques, may be used under the direction of a qualified physician, with no reduction in clinically significant diagnostic image quality. The types and ratios of compression used for different imaging studies transmitted and stored by the system should be selected and periodically reviewed by the responsible physician to ensure appropriate clinical image quality.

Transmission

The type and specifications of the transmission devices used will be dictated by the environment of the studies to be transmitted. In all cases, for official interpretation, the digital data received at the receiving end of any transmission must have no loss of clinically significant information. The transmission system shall have adequate error-checking capability.

Display Capabilities

Display workstations used for official interpretation and employed for small and large matrix systems should provide the following characteristics:

1. Luminance of the gray-scale monitors should be at least 50-foot lamberts
2. Lighting in the reading room should be controlled to eliminate reflections in the monitor and to lower the ambient lighting level as much as is possible
3. Capability for selecting image sequence
4. Capability for accurately associating the patient and study demographics characterizations with the study images
5. Capability of window and level adjustments, if those data are available
6. Capability of pan and zoom functions
7. Capability of rotating or flipping the images provided correct labeling of patient orientation is preserved
8. Capability of calculating and displaying accurate linear measurements and pixel value determinations in appropriate values for modality, such as Houndsfield units for CT images, if those data are available
9. Capability of displaying prior image compression ratio, processing, or cropping
10. The following elements of display should be available:
    1. Matrix size
    2. Bit depth
    3. Total number of images acquired in the study
    4. Clinically relevant technical parameters

When display systems are not used for the official interpretation, they need not meet all the characteristics listed above.

Archiving and Retrieval

If electronic archiving is to be employed, the guidelines listed below should be followed.

1. Teleradiology systems should provide storage capacity sufficient to comply with all facility, state, and federal regulations regarding medical record retention. Images stored at either site should meet the jurisdictional requirements of the transmitting site. Images interpreted offsite need not be stored at the receiving facility, provided they are stored at the transmitted site. However, if the images are retained at the receiving site, the retention period of that jurisdiction must be met as well. The policy on record retention must be in writing.
2. Each examination data file must have an accurate corresponding patient and examination database record, which includes patient name, identification, and facility at which the examination was performed. It is desirable that space be available for a brief clinical history.
3. Prior examinations should be retrievable from archives in a time frame appropriate to the clinical needs of the facility and medical staff.
4. Each facility should have policies and procedures for archiving and storage of digital image data equivalent to the policies for protection of hard-copy storage media to preserve imaging records.

Security

Teleradiology systems should provide network and software security protocols to protect the confidentiality of patients' identification and image data consistent with federal and state legal requirements. There should be measures to safeguard the data and to ensure integrity against intentional or unintentional corruption of the data.

Reliability and Redundancy

Quality patient care may depend on timely availability of the image interpretation. Written policies and procedures should be in place to ensure continuity of teleradiology services at a level consistent with those for hard-copy imaging studies and medical records within a facility or institution. This should include internal redundancy systems, backup communication links, and a disaster plan.

Licensing and Credentialing

Physicians who provide the official interpretation of images transmitted by teleradiology should maintain licensure as may be required for provisions of radiologic service at both the transmitting and receiving sites. When providing the official interpretation of images from a hospital, the physician should be credentialed and obtain appropriate privileges at the institution. These physicians should consult with their professional liability carrier to ensure coverage at both the sending and receiving sites, to include the state or jurisdiction.

The physician performing the official interpretation is responsible for the quality of the images being reviewed. The ACR Rules of Ethics state: "It is proper for a diagnostic radiologist to provide a consultative opinion on radiographs and other images regardless of their origin. A diagnostic radiologist should regularly interpret radiographs and other images only when the radiologist reasonably participates in the quality of medical imaging, utilization review, and matters of policy that affect the quality of patient care."

Images stored at either site (transmitting or receiving) should meet the jurisdictional requirements of the transmitting site. Jurisdictional requirements refer to federal, state, and local statutes. Images interpreted offsite need not be stored at the receiving facility, provided they are stored at the transmitting site. However, if images are retained at the receiving site, the retention period for that jurisdiction must be met as well. The policy on record retention should be in writing. The physicians who are involved in practicing teleradiology will conduct their practice in a manner consistent with the bylaws, rules, and regulations for patient care at the transmitting site.

Documentation

Communication is a critical component of teleradiology. Physicians interpreting teleradiology examinations should render reports in accordance with the ACR Standard for Communication: Diagnostic Radiology.

Quality Control and Improvement, Safety, Infection Control, and Patient Education Concerns

Policies and procedures related to quality, patient education, infection control, and safety should be developed and implemented in accordance with the ACR policies on Quality Control and Improvement, Safety, Infection Control, and Patient Education Concerns appearing in the ACR Standards Book.

Any facility using a teleradiology system must have documented policies and procedures for monitoring and evaluating the effective management, safety, and proper performance of acquisition, digitization, compression, transmission, archiving, and retrieval functions of the system. The quality control program should be designed to maximize the quality and accessibility of diagnostic information.

A test image, such as the SMPTE (Society of Motion Picture and Television Engineers) test pattern (SMPTE test pattern RP 133-1991, from Grey, J.F., Lisk, K.G., Haddick, D.H., et al., 1985. Test pattern for video displays and hard copy cameras. *Radiology* 154: 519–527), should be captured, transmitted, archived, retrieved, and displayed at appropriate intervals, but at least monthly, to test the overall operation of the system under conditions that simulate the normal operation of the system. As a spatial resolution test, at least 512 × 512 resolution should be confirmed for small matrix official interpretation, and 2.5 lp/mm resolutions for large matrix official interpretation.

As a test of the display, SMPTE pattern data files sized to occupy the full area used to display images on the monitor should be displayed. The overall SMPTE image appearance should be inspected to assure the absence of gross artifacts, such as blurring or bleeding of bright display areas into dark areas, or aliasing of spatial resolution patterns. Display monitors used for primary interpretation should be tested at least monthly. As a dynamic range test, both the 5 and the 95 percent areas should be seen as distinct from the respective adjacent 0 and 100 percent areas. The use of teleradiology does not reduce the responsibilities for the management and supervision of radiologic medicine.

(Reprinted pp. 135–142 with permission of the American College of Radiology. *ACR Standard for Teleradiology* listed in the Web site: *http://med.mc.ntw.edu. tw/~somed/teletea/document/teleradiology_standard.html*)

Legal Issues in Teleradiology

According to P. White in the article titled, "Legal Issues in Teleradiology-Distance Thoughts," *BJR*, 75: 202, 2002, legal issues may evolve with regards to liability, responsibility, accountability, and duty of care. The doctor–patient relationship is different in cases of teleradiology than with face-to-face consultations. In civil cases, a duty of care is usually owed if a patient has been accepted by the defendant and if issues of proximity and foreseeability can be established. When a patient requests medical services and a doctor undertakes to provide these services, then the legal relationship of doctor and patient will ensue. In teleradiology, it could be argued that the physician merely acts as a consultant and, therefore, has minimal contact with the patient. How the legal process would differentiate between such relationships is yet to be tested; however, what is clear is that the physician–patient relationship, with respect to proximity and responsibility, will need careful consideration. It will be important to clarify who maintains overall responsibility for the patient under these circumstances and, if, for example, clinical negligence is established, how liability would be apportioned according to the roles of the concerned parties.

Case law in *Diana L. Webb v. T.D. & C.H.A.*, No. 97-255, 951 P.2d, 1008; 1997, the Supreme Court of Montana, has already considered whether a physician who performs a medical examination of an individual at the request of a third party has a duty of care to the examinee and, if so, what the scope of that duty is. The defendant, in this case, claimed that he owed no duty of care, as he had no physician–patient relationship with the claimant. The Supreme Court judges held that the healthcare provider has a duty to exercise ordinary care to assure that when he/she advises an examinee about their condition following an independent examination, the advice comports with the standard of care for the healthcare provider's profession. It has also been suggested that if the radiologist's report becomes an official part of the patient's record, then it would be very unlikely that the court would find that no doctor–patient relationship had been established.

In *Bienz v. Central Suffolk Hospital*, 557 N.Y.S.2d, 139 (App. 1993), the court observed that if a doctor offers advice, treatment, or diagnosis over the telephone, a doctor–patient relationship is established. Therefore, the courts have developed a set of five questions to determine if a doctor–patient relationship exists:

1. Was there a meeting between the doctor and patient?
2. Did the doctor examine the patient?
3. Did the doctor review the patient's records?
4. Did the doctor know the patient's name?
5. Did the patient pay the doctor for services?

Only some of these questions must be answered in the affirmative in order to establish a doctor–patient relationship (Sivaswamy, R., et al. 2002. Doctors on the Internet—Legal and practical implications *Eubios Journal of Asian and International Bioethics* 12, 185–188).

In *Lopez v. Aziz*, 852, S.W.2d, 303 (Texas App. 1993), a doctor–patient relationship was not found when a consulting obstetrician talked to the patient's regular physician by phone. The court noted that because Aziz did not contact or examine Mrs. Lopez directly, and only spoke with her doctor, no relationship existed. Conversely, a relationship was found in *Wheeler v. Yettie Kersting Memorial Hospital*, 866, S.W.2d, 32 (Texas, APP. 1993), where an on-call physician used information obtained by phone regarding the status of a woman in labor to send the woman to a hospital. Because the doctor evaluated the patient's condition and recommended treatment over the telephone, the court found that a doctor–patient relationship existed. Even though a patient may not be in the same room with a doctor, a relationship may still be formed by the use of telemedicine to diagnose or treat a patient. A related problem is in determining where malpractice liability lies in a telemedicine scenario. There is a problem in determining joint or independent liability for all the physicians involved, the referring physician who is at the same location as the patient, and the physician consulting via telemedicine (Sivaswamy et al. 2002).

Case laws will suggest that a doctor's participation in telemedicine consultations, whether or not his or her advice is followed, establishes a doctor–patient relationship. In *Greenberg v. Perkins*, 845, P.2d, 530 (Colorado, 1993), the court held that even if a traditional doctor–patient relationship is not present, a physician who examines a nonpatient still has a duty not to cause harm to the person being examined.

Another issue related to teleradiology malpractice involves the applicable jurisdiction in which the lawsuit should be filed. In a situation where there exists a transboundary consultation, the question of jurisdiction becomes important. Therefore, to determine jurisdiction, courts must first determine where the practice of medicine was committed. Exercising personal jurisdiction is contingent on two requirements. First, in *International Shoe Co. v. Washington*, 326, U.S. 310 (1945), a nonresident defendant must have purposefully availed himself of the benefits and protections of the state by establishing minimum contracts with the state. Second, in *Asahi Metal Indus. Co. v. Superior Court*, 480, U.S. 102 (1987), exercising such jurisdiction must not offend traditional notions of fair play and substantial justice.

In *Wright v. Yackley*, 459, F. 2d, 287 (9th Cir. 1972), a malpractice action involving an Idaho patient and a South Dakota doctor resulted in a ruling that proper jurisdiction lay in South Dakota because all diagnoses and prescriptions were made in that state. The patient, a former South Dakota resident, could not claim Idaho jurisdiction because the malpractice action arose from the confirmation of an old prescription. However, the court noted that had the treatment been a new one rather than the continuance of a prior visit, the jurisdiction of the patient's state might also be controlling. The court ultimately ruled that the focus must be on the place where services are rendered. Based on such rulings, a doctor practicing telemedicine may need to be aware of laws and regulations in other states that may have jurisdiction over his activities, particularly in the area of physician licensing (Sivaswamy et al. 2002).

Clinical negligence comes under the auspices of tort law, whereby private or personal injury to a person or property may result in damages being claimed in a court of law. The civil law provides for compensation to a person injured by another's negligence, and this is the usual avenue of redress for patient's taking legal action within the healthcare system. The patient will claim that the doctor was negligent because of breach of duty to exercise reasonable care and skill in diagnosing, advising, or treating the patient.

In conventional radiology, the radiologist must examine the patient, if necessary; however, in teleradiology, the radiologist may also have a duty to warn the patient that the lack of opportunity to physically examine the patient may increase the risk of misdiagnosis. Fundamentally, there are four models in teleradiology, which are

1. Telediagnosis: Typically, this service involves asynchronous point-to-point communication and requires relatively simple applications and a minimum of infrastructure. In response to a request by a remote site, which transmits all or selected images of a diagnostic examination, specialists at a major medical center review these images and return a diagnostic report to the requesting site. Telediagnosis is particularly useful for rural and other areas that are not well served by specialized medical personnel.

2. Telemonitoring: In most modern diagnostic imaging procedures, patient positioning and the process of image acquisition are important factors determining diagnostic image quality. Telemonitoring serves the need for expert

supervision of image acquisition by a specific imaging modality. Furthermore, an expert can manipulate and view image data during the examination, therefore, being able to request additional images after issuing instructions on how to reposition the patient or adjust the imaging parameters. Telemonitoring does not impose heavy demands on the application layer, as the transactions between different sites are of a simple nature. Specifically, video sequences of the examination room and the patient are transmitted to the expert who monitors the procedure and interacts with the examination site through an image and voice data link. However, the requirement for real-time multimedia communication imposes additional technological demands on the available infrastructure.

3. Teleconsultation: In recent years, the number and complexity of biological signals, which can be recorded and also presented in the form of reconstructed images, has increased substantially. This has given rise to the need for subspecialization, which has resulted in an increased demand for consultation among different medical experts. Providing a shared workplace among medical experts at remote and distant locations is one of the main functions of the teleconsultation service. This service requires the synchronous viewing and manipulation of the same set of radiological images and other patient data, as well as the real-time exchange of comments among all parties involved in the session. It is evident that the synchronization of the media and procedures involved in a teleconsultation session requires various types of complex transactions and resource management mechanisms, therefore, imposing serious demands on the underlying applications. Furthermore, the real-time nature of the service and the volume of multimedia data exchange require a technologically advanced infrastructure.

4. Telemanagement: The combination of advanced telemonitoring and teleconsultation services, with remote resource sharing, offers the possibility for the telematic management of diagnostic and therapeutic procedures. This teleradiology service will gain momentum in the future with parallel developments in the areas of virtual reality, 3D video communications, and telepresence. It may then become possible for teleradiology to also support remote diagnostic imaging examinations, as well as image-guided radiation therapy and surgery (Excerpts from Orphanoudakis et al. 1996).

Data acquisition and manipulation issues are key factors for consideration in terms of image quality and diagnosis. The development of digital imaging has required radiologists to adopt new skills to overcome the potential for image degradation during the process of digitization and transmission of nondigital images. However, there is a responsibility to ensure that the equipment is fit for the purpose for which it is used. From a legal standpoint, it would be negligent to produce and examine images of substandard quality by reason of inferior equipment or resulting from variable operator dependency, such as lack of experience in interpreting images by these methods. Consequently, any errors in diagnosis arising from such practice may be entitled to compensation. Therefore, the advantages of teleradiology are only relevant if images are of sufficient quality without significant loss of spatial or contrast resolution from image acquisition through transmission to final image display.

There have always been questions regarding the accuracy of diagnosis with digital imaging and how this may impact on the malpractice issues of teleradiology. There have been major advancements in film digitization; however, it must be decided in a court of law whether there has been any degradation of the image during image transmission, and whether this has impacted on the accuracy of the diagnosis. There may be further concerns that the operators of the digital process may also lack the experience to achieve the optimal viewing conditions and, in this case, the defendants would have to establish their competence to use the equipment. It has been consistently held in case law that inexperience is no defense for clinical negligence or malpractice.

If the patient were to establish, on a balance of probabilities, that the defendant's failure to promptly provide treatment would have accentuated the harm suffered and represented breach of duty, then the patient would be entitled to compensation for the harm that occurred. It would not be too unrealistic to argue that digital radiology should speed up the reporting process in situations where the images need to be sent to a radiologist or specialist at a distant site.

To reduce exposure to malpractice liability, the participants in the teleradiology network should consider creating written policies that address the following:

1. Have adequate and appropriate documentation. The local and consulting providers document and record the patients' histories, examination, diagnosis, treatments, and recommendations.
2. Providers should clarify and document the equipment to be used, the parties responsible for equipment maintenance, the format of transmitting medical information, the studies to be interpreted, the hours of coverage, the frequency and format of reports, quality assurance mechanisms, and important staffing issues. The duties and responsibilities of each party involved, in a teleradiology arrangement, should be clearly defined in a written contract. Indemnification provisions also should be included.
3. Practitioners providing medical services through teleradiology must meet the standard of care (the national standard of care) associated with the type of service provided and the standard of care for providing those services via telecommunications.
4. Transmission verification procedures should be established at both the local and remote sites.
5. Create contingency plans. Every provider should have a written policy or guidelines establishing a course of action for emergencies, including when

there is a power outage, equipment malfunction, or other unforeseen incident that interferes with the teleradiology network.

6. The network should promulgate clinical guidelines and protocols. These guidelines and protocols should be realistic. If the practitioner or entity fails to meet these guidelines or protocols, such failure may support a finding by the court that there was a deviation from the proper standard of care.

7. Regarding record storage, retention, and maintenance, the teleradiology business must comply with the federal and state law requirements.

8. Each party involved in the teleradiology network should be required to carry insurance in the event of an error or malfunction. Teleradiology consultants should confirm whether their professional liability insurance policies cover liability in the patients' states for services provided from outside these states via teleradiology.

9. Teleradiology entities should ensure that their employees and independent contractors are properly credentialed, privileged, and accredited with respect to their abilities to provide medical care and to use telemedical equipment.

10. The providers should thoroughly investigate the vendors providing the hardware and software products and services to determine if they are sound and experienced, and whether they honor their support and maintenance contracts and provide appropriate training. Because the practitioners will most likely be held liable for patient harm resulting from failing to use the teleradiology equipment reasonably, the practitioner should routinely inspect the equipment to make sure it functions properly, confirm that the vendor will service and maintain the equipment on an ongoing basis, and ensure that the system will permit the patients' records to be reasonably protected and allow the practitioner to obtain patient information during a system failure.

11. The vendor's responsibility should be identified in writing and include what services are to be provided, upgrades, costs, training, maintenance, support, and indemnification.

(Excerpts from Cepelwicz, B.B. June 2003. Telelegalities. Journal of Imaging Technologies Management. Web site: http://www.imagingeconomics.com/library/tools/printengine.asp?printArticleID=200306-13)

Security and Confidentiality

The management of medical records, including radiographic film and other hardcopy images, may be an additional problem with teleradiology and computerized patient records. Security issues relating to increased risk of improper disclosure of records, breach of confidentiality, access to records, alteration or elimination of records from a remote site, vulnerability of computer-stored data to accidental erasure, and methods of ensuring verification are the concerns that must be addressed. There are three issues relating to data security. They include:

1. Privacy, which determines who can access the data security
2. Authenticity, which determines who sends the data
3. Integrity, which determines whether the data has been altered during its transmission through public networks

It has been suggested that the first two issues are the responsibility of the data centers or technology services of the sender and the receiver. Privacy and authenticity can be resolved using various levels of passwords, based on a balance between convenience and cost. Integrity is the responsibility of the site where the image is generated and this may not be so easy to protect. Encryption of data is one method to protect the data. However, there is a concern about the security of data held on a computer and transmitted between sites. To protect individuals, it is essential to remove personal identifiers or to encrypt transmitted information.

The law has not been able to keep pace with teleradiology and is a testing ground for many legal and practical issues. Nevertheless, some states have formulated laws governing these issues. California requires licensed providers who use electronic systems to comply with certain regulations, including offsite backup data storage systems, safeguards for confidentiality and unauthorized access, authentication by electronic signature keys, and guidelines for system maintenance (Excerpts from White, P. 2002).

Political Considerations and Turf Issues

Teleradiology is mired with turf battles and intermedicine conflicts. Some radiologists fear that managed care plans will use teleradiology to establish networks that would shut out local radiologists, or that hospitals may replace local radiologists with out-of-state teleradiology groups. These fears are fueled by the emergence of teleradiology companies that have been formed to offer their services, often in competition with local radiologists, in both rural and metropolitan areas throughout the United States. Such fears are reinforced by a recent *Wall Street Journal* article that reported the creation of a joint venture between a Texas-based university and a communications company that will take advantage of a diverging trend in medicine, including the rise of managed care and the development of technology that will enable the delivery of high quality, digitized x-ray images (Excerpts from Berlin, L. 1998. Malpractice issues in radiology, *American Journal of Radiology*, 170: 1417–1422).

In an article titled, Teleradiology by Lee, C.D., from *Radiology*, 1996, 201: 15, a California radiologist reported that a few powerful and greedy individuals and groups are destroying practices of local community or rural radiologists under the guise of being able to offer a better and, in some cases, more economical service. They are not able to interact with clinicians, attend medical staff and community meetings, or perform other hospital functions. W. J. Casarella, established in Benefits of Teleradiology (1996) from *Radiology*, 201: 16–17, that teleradiology allows the transmission of images in difficult cases to those members of a group best trained to interpret them. He indicated that teleradiology is here, it works, and it will only get easier, better, and cheaper (Excerpts from Berlin, L. 1998).

Suspicion that teleradiologic groups will place the livelihood of local radiologists in jeopardy cannot be denied among segments of the radiologic community. Mistrust and animosity are natural consequences of such suspicions. However, the continued growth of teleradiology is likely to generate increasing ferocity of turf battles among radiologists.

Teleradiology is an offspring of the computer age. Technologic innovations in acquiring and transmitting radiologic images have propelled teleradiology from an uncertain infancy to a proven approach. The increasing use and expanding applications of teleradiology are likely to continue in an unabated fashion; however, at the same time, they are likely to be accompanied by a corresponding growth of malpractice litigations, such as medical licensure, physician–patient relationships, accuracy, jurisdiction, standards, and turf battles.

Review Questions

1. What are the goals of teleradiology?
   1. Provide consultive service.
   2. Facilitate radiology interpretations in on-call situations.
   3. Provide subspecialty support.
   4. Provide supervision of onsite imaging studies.
      a. 1 and 2
      b. 3 and 4
      c. 1, 2, and 3
      d. 1, 2, 3, and 4

2. When using a small matrix size, what is the minimum pixel depth required for processing the teleradiographic image at the display monitor?
   a. 2-bit
   b. 8-bit
   c. 10-bit
   d. 12-bit

3. What individual must be qualified to assess and provide problem-solving input to assure sustainable high image quality and system function?
   a. Radiologic technologist
   b. Medical physicist
   c. Physician
   d. Image management specialist

4. The quality control program should be designed to maximize the quality and accessibility of diagnostic information.
   a. True
   b. False

Chapter 12

Forensic Radiology

Upon completion of Chapter 12, the reader will be able to:

1. Apply radiographic technique to determine cause of death.
2. Define battered child syndrome.
3. Identify signs of child abuse.
4. Discuss the legal implications toward child abuse.

Forensic Radiology

The first forensic use of radiology in locating metallic objects in criminal cases was done in January, 1896, four months after Wilhelm Roentgen discovered the x-ray.

A Mrs. Hartley of Nelson, England, was shot in the head by her husband who then drowned himself in the Liverpool canal. He fired four shots into the head of his wife. Doctor William Little, general practitioner, and Arthur Schuster, physics professors at Owens College in Manchester, tried to locate the bullets utilizing the newly discovered roentgen ray (x-ray).

The first exposure was noted as taking one hour in duration and the second exposure, 70 minutes. Dr. Schuster developed the bariumplatanocide plates and located three bullets inside the cranium of Mrs. Hartley.

The procedure that Dr. Schuster performed was using the Crooks' tube. He brought three tubes to the house; he had two tubes as spares. He had a DC generator and glass photographic plates. There was no main electricity. The local company provided storage batteries to provide power.

According to documentation, one of the assistants to Dr. Schuster suffered a nervous breakdown attributed to the radiograph of the mutilated and dying woman. It took a total of 10 days to set up the apparatus and radiograph Mrs. Hartley. She died on May 9, 1896, 15 days after receiving the gunshot wounds.

This is documented in the *Nelson and Colne Express*, which was the local newspaper (Knight and Evans, 1981).

Forensic radiology is used to:

1. Determine whether bones are actually present, whether they are human, and to determine basic features, such as age, sex, and stature.
2. Compare two sets of radiographs, antemortem versus postmortem views. A person's fingerprints are not the only parts of the anatomy that can be used for investigative purposes. Both dental and skeletal films are useful because no two person's teeth or skeletons are exactly alike. Forensic dentistry is comparing antemortem and postmortem dental films. This is the best known and widely used technique in forensic medicine. Almost everyone has had dental x-rays taken within the past five years, and the teeth are among the best preserved of the body parts, even in a fire. Apart from the teeth and jaws, the most helpful part of the body for comparison radiography is the skull. The skull has many characteristic features, especially the paranasal sinuses. Other useful features are peculiarities of bony architecture and unique trabecular patterns. The cervical spine, vascular grooves, clavicle, lumbar spine, skeletal deformities, angulations, callus formation, congenital abnormalities, unique abnormalities, such as a dorsal defect of the patella, and the ossification patterns in the costal cartilage of the first rib are good areas for comparison.
3. Identify bodies with previous antemortem injuries. An old chest film may be the only antemortem x-ray available on a John or Jane Doe. However, in the upper corner of that film might be an old fracture of the clavicle that can be compared to the body in question. Foreign bodies, such as old bullets or shrapnel, are also helpful. Besides anatomical differences, prosthetics, synthetic joints, hip replacement, pacemakers, surgical implants, and disease processes make for easy identification.

Determining Cause of Death

Radiographic imaging techniques are also helpful in determining cause of death. Death caused by a penetrating wound, strangulation, drowning, electrical shock, metallic poison, and/or blast injuries can be easily determined radiographically. In multiple-injury cases, radiographs will enable the radiologists to discover which wound was fatal. If a large caliber shotgun wound is made to the head, the skull will fracture and there is massive brain trauma.

Imaging Techniques

Plain film radiography is the imaging technique most commonly employed by forensic radiologists for identification and/or discovering the cause of death. Other imaging modalities are used in special circumstances.

A fluoroscopic unit can be employed by the medical examiner to recover foreign objects, such as needles and bullets, from bodies. Angiography is used to study vessel injuries. This is especially useful when investigating "surgical misadventures" and other iatrogenic problems. It is a law in San Francisco that all patients who die unexpectedly in hospitals must be examined by the coroner. All tubes and other equipment must be left in place. The bodies are studied for tube ruptures, catheter perforations, and other possible causes of death, often with the aid of angiography.

Forensic angiographic techniques must be modified slightly when working on corpses because of the absence of blood circulation and washout, which is the elimination of the contrast agent. Positional and scout films are taken to define the region of interest. Because there is no washout, only one injection of media contrast is possible, making it vital that the procedure be done properly.

A large load of contrast is delivered via pressure injector in one end of the vessels under examination and pumped out at the other end. Utilizing large amounts of contrast media will produce very clear and useful images. Most medical examiners and forensic radiologists use imaging equipment at county hospitals or employ the services of portable x-ray companies. If hospital facilities are used for forensic studies, the areas are disinfected after use.

Battered Child Syndrome

Radiology can play a vital role in the confirmation of the diagnosis of child abuse. Clinical examinations may reveal evidence of neglect, but a carefully conducted radiological exam can disclose not only the etiology of bone lesions, but may give information on the approximate ages, number, and sites of bone abnormalities.

Battered child syndrome is defined as the radiologic appearance of bizarre and unusual injuries of the bones in affected children. These presumably result from repetitive trauma due to unawareness or deliberate denial on the part of those responsible. Radiographic evidence of the battered child syndrome, such as fractures of different ages in the same child, is accepted proof of abuse by the courts.

Perhaps the most telling sign of abuse is multiple skeletal injuries at different stages of healing. Classical radiographic findings indicating nonaccidental injuries are epiphyseal and metaphyseal fractures. Injuries to the metaphysis, and spiral and transverse fractures of the long bones may result from swinging the baby or child and forcefully wrenching or twisting the limbs.

Uncommon fracture sites, such as the lateral end of the clavicle, are usually encountered only following perinatal trauma or child abuse. Shaking or twisting probably produces such an injury. Sternal and scapular fractures are also suspect, as is thickening of the cortex and of periosteal elevation. Rib fractures are also uncommon in childhood. Such fractures are frequently bilateral due to side-to-side pressure from adult hands grasping the child around the thorax and squeezing during shaking.

Brain trauma, subdural hematoma, and cerebral edema are the most common serious and urgent complications of nonaccidental skull injuries. This is often caused by whiplash from shaking the child. Radiography can provide supportive evidence for subdural hematoma by demonstrating separated cranial bones and widened sutures, other signs of increased intracranial pressure, or obvious fractures of the cranial bones.

Other suspicious head injuries include absence of hair or hemorrhaging beneath the scalp due to vigorous hair pulling, retinal hemorrhages, and jaw and nasal fractures. Abdominal injuries compose about 25 percent of the total injuries in child abuse. Injuries include duodenal and jejunal hematomas, rupture of the inferior vena cava, splenic rupture, renal rupture, gastric rupture, perforation of both intra- and extraperitoneal organs, peritonitis, soft tissue edema, intramural hematomas of the alimentary tract, pancreatic injury, pancreatitis, and general bruising, all of which can be documented by radiography.

Plain films of the abdomen reveal free gas or fluid in the peritoneal cavity or signs of peritonitis. Other radiographic evidence of visceral trauma includes pneumoperitoneum and/or ileus.

It must be remembered that suspicious injuries can be caused by other conditions. Some diseases also mimic abuse, such as scurvy, osteogenesis imperfecta, congenital syphilis, and infantile cortical hyperostosis.

The radiographer can gain useful information for the doctor by producing good quality radiographs for diagnostic interpretation. More importantly, the radiographer can gain the confidence of the child by being caring, honest, and friendly. In a friendly environment, the child may state the truth in how he/she was injured. The child may respond to questions better if he/she is not frightened when he/she enters the radiology department.

State laws require healthcare providers to report abuse to a child protection agency, such as the police or sheriff's department, county probation, or county welfare department. The Child Abuse Reporting Law specifically provides that neither the physician–patient privilege nor the psychotherapist–patient privilege applies to any information reported pursuant to this law. Not only is failure to report a criminal offense, but it is also a grave breach of professional responsibility to both the child and parent.

Hospital staff, including radiographers, should be familiar with the indicators of child abuse. Medical personnel should also be alert to "hospital shoppers." These are people who, for no apparent reason, have brought an injured child to a hospital outside of their community when their own community has fully equipped facilities. Often, this is done to cover up a pattern of abuse because medical records sometimes reveal a history of hospital and doctor "shopping" that may, in conjunction with other indicators, be indicative of suspected abuse.

According to the law, specified medical personnel or their agents may take skeletal x-rays of a child for purposes of diagnosing and determining the extent of possible child abuse without the consent of the parent or guardian. Medical professionals and other mandated reporters may be subject to civil damage suits if they fail to report suspected child abuse.

In the case of *Landeros v. Flood* (1976) Cal. 3d 399, an infant, Gina, was brought into a hospital with injuries, treated and released back to her mother. Subsequently, she was treated for new and more serious injuries by a second doctor, who reported the injuries as suspected child abuse. The child was made a dependent of the court and a guardian *ad litem* was appointed. The guardian *ad litem* then instituted a suit on behalf of the child against the first doctor for failure to report as required by law. The California Supreme Court reversed a lower court decision, which dismissed the complaint, and held that the complaint stated a cause of action based on a failure to report as required by statute. The case held that failure to perform the statutorily imposed duty to report raises a presumption that a defendant doctor failed to exercise due care. The Supreme Court sent the case back to the lower court for trial. The plaintiffs in this case sued the doctor for $2 million, plus costs. A decision for the plaintiffs would obviously have been serious for the doctor involved. In spite of the ultimate outcome of this case (the charges could not be substantiated), it is clear that health practitioners and other healthcare providers who have a statutory duty to report may be held civilly as well as criminally liable when they fail to report suspected cases as required by law.

The importance of law enforcement's role in child abuse cases centers on the fact that child abuse is a crime, and that the primary consideration is for the protection of the child. Reports of suspected child abuse must be made to the police or sheriff's departments, or other designated child protective agencies. Law enforcement personnel are also best trained to ensure protection of constitutional rights and due process procedures during the course of the investigation.

The responding officer will decide whether to take the child into temporary custody, to arrest the parents/caretakers, to seek the filing of criminal charges, or to refer the case to child welfare services or another appropriate agency. Final disposition should be made after consultation with representatives of other disciplines.

As in all other areas of criminal law, all searches, seizures, and arrests made in the course of child abuse investigations must comply with the requirements of the Fourth Amendment.

According to the U.S. Department of Human Services, Administration for Children and Families reported in 2005 that 803,000 children were victims of child abuse. These figures make it necessary that healthcare professionals, including radiographers, become more aware of abnormalities that may point toward child abuse.

Appendix A

Situations

Insurance Situation

You are a staff radiographer performing emergency procedures during an "on-call shift." Risk management data indicate that emergency on-call procedures are an area of high legal liability. You are concerned about your malpractice liability coverage. In discussing this issue with your radiology administrator, she states, "There is no need to worry — we have been told that all radiography staff is covered by the hospital insurance."

What, if any, are some legal risks involved?

Answer

Today we are all concerned about insurance. It is the civilized method of distributing risk. Most of us pay required premiums for health insurance, car insurance, life insurance, and homeowners insurance. In fact, if one wanted — or could afford — to deal with Lloyds of London, one could have his hands or voice or any precious possessions insured for a sufficient premium.

Insurance is a contract or agreement by which an insurer agrees to assume certain risks of the insured for a premium. The insurer agrees to pay the insured, or certain persons, a specific amount of money if an event occurs for which one is covered.

Insurance policies are usually elaborate as most laymen know. In fact, lawyers will advise that the best way of reviewing a policy is just to read the fine print. An insurance policy will contain the identification of the risk involved, the specified occurrence, and the specific amount payable should the event occur.

When analyzing an insurance policy, there are five distinct parts one should always review to have a better understanding of the actual coverage one has. The insurance agreement states what the insurer assumes to pay, or his legal liability, but not any moral obligations. There is the policy period, which clearly states that period of time when the policy is in effect. There is a defense and settlement clause that defines how the company will defend the insured against suit and its power to settle claims against the insured. The insurance policy will have a clause stating the amount of money the insured person will pay, how it will be paid, and the maximum amount of money the insured person will pay for the policy. Finally, one of the most important sections of the policy is the condition under which the policy will be paid. There are always important conditions in each liability contract, and failure to comply with those stated conditions could result in the policy's being forfeited or canceled. An insurance policy is a contract with legal obligations on both sides between the insured and the insurer. Failure to meet those conditions by either party is a breach of the contract.

By risk, one means there is a possibility some type of loss may occur. There are generally three categories of risk to which an individual is exposed. There is the risk to property where one incurs loss or damage; there is the risk to person, such as injury to health or life; and there is risk to one's profession or legal liability, such as malpractice.

Insurance protection starts immediately when the agent gives the insured a binder. If no binder has been obtained from the agent, the insurance is generally not effective until the policy is delivered to the insured.

Obviously, it is difficult for the average person or family to bear the cost of serious damage to health, property, or person. Insurance is based on the principle that categories of persons exposed to the same type of risk or hazard pay premiums into a general fund from which the insured will be indemnified in the event the risk event occurs.

The professional liability insurance policies give standard coverage using a clause, such as: "To pay on behalf of the insured all sums that the insured shall become legally obligated to pay as damages because of injury arising out of malpractice, or error in rendering or failing to render, radiographic services."

Do radiographers need to carry their own malpractice insurance? The answer, of course, depends on many factors that can only be judged by the individual radiographer who can weigh all the factors and make an intelligent decision. However, the author wishes to point out that few, if any, persons today would be without health insurance or automobile insurance. The risk involved in being without coverage is frightening to all of us. We are all aware of persons who did not have adequate coverage and whose financial resources were wiped out by lengthy illnesses. So, it would seem well worth the small premium for radiographers to carry professional liability insurance.

At present, the average malpractice insurance premium for radiographers costs about $85 per year for $1 to $3 million in liability coverage. That seems a small price to pay for peace of mind. Another observation is that, as long as one finds the premiums so low, it indicates that the lawsuits are not numerous. It is logical to assume that there is a direct relationship between the cost of premiums and the risk involved.

Why do radiographers need individual liability insurance? There is no assurance that a radiographer will not be sued individually even though covered or partially covered by the hospital or agency for whom he/she works. Also, even though the employer may be liable under the doctrine of respondeat superior for actions of the radiographer, the employer, through the insurance company, may file a claim against the radiographer to get back money paid out. This is called subrogating the claim. The insurance company "stands in the shoes" of the employer. In fact, most insurance policies contain a subrogation clause, which permits the insurance company to sue appropriate parties to regain any monies paid out under the insurance agreement. The radiographer can always be held liable for his/her own actions, whether named alone or as a co-defendant.

Malpractice liability insurance pays the court-awarded verdict and the cost of legal counsel. If you procure a $50,000/$150,000 policy, this means your insurance company will pay a maximum of $50,000 in damages to any one person injured as a result of your malpractice, and it will pay a maximum of $150,000 in damages in any one year on all claims against the radiographer.

Healthcare is a high-risk area for most of us. With advanced technology, educated patients, and increased risk of lawsuits, the radiographer must be fully aware of what coverage he/she has, and what coverage he/she needs, to be protected adequately in the event he/she must defend himself/herself in a lawsuit.

The malpractice risk for radiographers is significant and recent indications are that the risks will increase in importance. Practically all persons involved in the radiographic field face the risk of a malpractice suit. A majority of radiographers recognize the significance of the risk exposure; those who have not done so should objectively examine their potential risk. The amount and limits of malpractice insurance should be commensurate with the risk of the radiographer, hospital, or health agency.

Vignette 23

Teaching Environment Situation

Sally Solenoid is scheduled for a mammographic procedure. Doctor Angstrom, who is interpreting the mammographic films, decides to perform a breast examination on Solenoid. Prior to this examination, he asks three radiography students to observe the breast examination?

What, if any, are some legal risks involved?

Answer

There is often a misconception among health professionals that a patient who is admitted to a teaching hospital automatically becomes a subject for teaching, learning, and practicing procedures. This is not correct. Patients do not waive any rights, constitutional or otherwise, because they are treated in an institution that also educates radiographers. It is appropriate for the patient to be informed of who is attending her and under what conditions. All parties working with, and for, the patient should introduce and identify himself or herself by name and position to the patient. The patient always has the option of refusing the procedure, either the procedure itself or the person purporting to perform the procedure.

The law is clear that admission of nonessential persons during procedures and treatments of a patient constitutes a violation of the right of privacy unless the patient has given consent.

Each of the parties, that is, Dr. Angstrom and the three radiography students, would be at legal risk for invading the patient's privacy if the breast examination is for the radiography student's benefit and not for the patient's benefit, and the patient has not been consulted regarding the examination. The patient also has the right to be examined and treated by licensed, competent, and trained healthcare professionals. If less qualified persons are to be attending the patient, the patient should be made aware of this fact. It is then up to the patient to accept or reject the particular staff. Each time a patient is subjected to another unnecessary examination, it means added inconvenience and additional radiation exposure. Radiography students are learning and, therefore, presumably not as academically competent and not as skilled at technique as licensed radiographers. We are living in an era of the consumer's right to know. Certainly, in the area of healthcare, the patient should be fully informed.

Vignette 24

Protecting Personal Property

Amy Ampere, R.T., is the evening radiography supervisor in a small community hospital. Marie Matter is admitted to the hospital complaining of vomiting and diarrhea. Matter has been admitted to the medical floor with a tentative diagnosis of food poisoning. On the way to her room, she is sent to the radiology department for a chest x-ray. Matter was transported to her bed after the completion of the chest x-ray.

While the nurse was taking her T.P.R. and blood pressure, Matter indicated that her diamond wedding ring that had been on her left hand is missing. She established that the ring is worth $500 and wants it back immediately or she is going to sue the hospital for negligence in caring for her and her property.

Who, if anyone, is liable? What principles of law, if any, are involved? Is the hospital responsible for the patient's property? Would there be a different outcome if the patient were unconscious?

Answer

It is the general policy in most healthcare facilities to have a place available for safekeeping of any valuable articles. Upon admission, the patient should have been asked if she had any valuables that she would want placed in the hospital safe. If there is family present, the patient should be given the option of entrusting any valuables to the family. The hospital and the radiography personnel have an obligation to exercise reasonable care in protecting the patient's money and valuables.

Reasonable care requires that the hospital provide a safe place and notify the patient of the opportunity to place valuables there.

The hospital or radiography personnel cannot guarantee that the patient's possessions will not be stolen. They only promise to provide reasonable security. The patient was conscious when admitted and in control of her possessions. The patient has a duty to act as a reasonably prudent person at all times. It would be prudent for the patient to take the precaution of notifying the hospital personnel of the ring and of the approximate value and request that the article be placed in a safe.

When property is entrusted to the hospital for safekeeping, a bailment relationship takes place. Bailment is the delivering of personal property to another for a specific purpose. The bailor is the person who delivers the property. The bailee is the one to whom the property is delivered. When the purpose for the bailment is achieved, the bailee returns the article to the bailor. The bailee must take responsible care of the property entrusted to him and is liable for loss or damage to the property caused by his negligence.

The radiographer should create the necessary documentation and have a witness verify the specific amount, if money is involved, and the specific article if rings, watches, or other valuable articles are involved.

If the patient is unconscious, the radiographer would have a higher duty to protect the patient's possessions. On admission to any unit, part of the admission procedure should be a protocol for covering patient's belongings. However, if articles are missing from the patient and the radiographer had no knowledge of the incident, neither the radiographer nor the hospital will be held liable. The standard of care is ordinary and reasonable and as long as the radiographer acts as a reasonably prudent person would act in a similar situation.

When a patient is admitted to the hospital he/she often brings several types of personal property. Property can have monetary value, such as money, rings, or watches. Or, property can be of a personal nature, such as false teeth, eyeglasses, contact lenses, or other prostheses. Also, property can have a religious or sentimental value, such as a Bible, medals, or crosses.

It is incumbent on the hospital and the hospital administrator to maintain an environment of safety and security for the patient and the patient's property. The law applied here is that of bailment. The patient has the right to expect that any property entrusted to the hospital's care through the agency of personnel working there will be returned intact. The hospital administration is not responsible for any property of which it has no knowledge. However, if any property, which has been deposited for safekeeping, is damaged or missing, the hospital would be liable.

There are certain precautions regarding property that reasonably prudent patients should take. Patients are bound by the "reasonably prudent man" doctrine. Therefore, the patient should not bring valuable property to a healthcare facility because no healthcare facility can guarantee that nothing will happen to property in the complicated matrix system of a hospital. If the patient is admitted under circumstances in which he could not foresee or make preparations for the valuables on him, the valuables should be given to a spouse or member of the family, with appropriate documentation of the event, such as a receipt from the family member.

Vignette 25

Search and Seizure

Cathy Caliper, R.T., was working the 3 to 11 p.m. shift and, on a particular evening, a male patient, Benny Beam, was sent to the radiology department from the emergency room accompanied by two police officers. Caliper was order to perform multiple radiographs on Beam. One of the police officers, Andy Anode, asked Caliper to search the clothes and belongings of Beam while he was on the x-ray table during the radiographic procedure. The police officer wanted the radiographer to locate narcotics that were believed to be in Beam's possession.

Cathy Caliper wanted to be cooperative with the police officer, but was not sure what legal risks were involved.

Should Cathy Caliper comply with the request to search for drugs the patient may have in his possession? What, if any, legal liability could result?

Answer

The Fourth Amendment of the Constitution of the United States indicates "the right of the people to be secure in their persons, houses, papers, and effects, against unreasonable searches and seizures shall not be violated, and no warrants shall issue, but upon probable cause, supported by oath or affirmation, and particularly describing the place to be searched, and the persons or things to be seized." The Constitution confers certain rights on all of its citizens. The Fourth Amendment confers the right to be left alone, to be free from warrantless intrusions, to have privacy, to be secure in one's person and one's personal effects. This is not an absolute right, but is a qualified right. This means the Fourth Amendment does not confer an absolute right of prohibiting all searches and seizures. It gives the protection of a qualified right and prohibits all unreasonable searches of a person or a person's personal effects.

In the landmark case of *Mapp v. Ohio,* 367 U.S. (1961), the Supreme Court ruled that any evidentiary material taken in an unreasonable search cannot be used against the person from whom it was improperly obtained in any court of law. This is called the exclusionary rule of evidence because such evidence is selectively excluded in a trial on the merits of the case involving such information or physical evidence.

The history of cases related to search has established that it is a fundamental rule that a search without a warrant is not reasonable unless an arrest is involved. If an individual is to be searched without a warrant, or without the individual consenting to the search, there must be an arrest. The general rule is that if the search precedes the arrest, and the search provides the basis or probable cause, the search would be *ipso facto* an unreasonable search.

The courts recognize the police officer's right to seize instruments, contraband, and the fruits of crime that are in plain view. This is referred to as the plain view doctrine. In the present case, one main issue is that the patient, Benny Beam, is not under arrest. If the patient was under arrest, police officer Anode would be justified in searching the arrestee, his clothing, and personal effects. These same articles could be subjected to forensic laboratory conditions.

A warrant must describe the person, place, and things to be searched or seized with a reasonable degree of specificity. An exception to the general rule of requiring a warrant prior to searching an individual is where there are exigent circumstances and a clear indication that evidence has been seized. An example would be after a car collision or accident: the arresting officer can search the individual and the immediate area, but not the trunk of the car.

The patients, of course, could give expressed consent to search, effectively waiving their fundamental right of protection as guaranteed by the Fourth Amendment. This waiver would have to be completely voluntary and understood to be an intentional waiver of their constitutional right.

The Fourth Amendment does not protect abandoned property, but there is nothing abandoned in the present case. There is in the law the theory of custodial safety. In a 1960 federal court case, it was held that the law does not require a warrant to search and seize an object or article from an incarcerated person, which could be used by a prisoner to harm himself or others. This case involved the protection of a prisoner and a prisoner's property (*Charles v. U.S.*, 278F. 2d 286 [1960]).

The conclusion to be drawn is that, as a general rule, the healthcare provider does not have the authority, the right, or the responsibility to search the patient. However, as with all, there is a common sense exception. It may happen that while caring for a patient, it comes to the attention of the healthcare provider that the patient has a weapon, such as a knife or gun, or a large amount of drugs. If reasonable healthcare providers concluded from the known fact that the patient may harm others or himself with the weapon or drugs, then the healthcare provider has a duty to act to protect the patient and other potential victims. The healthcare provider must take action as is commensurate with the imminent danger to the safety and well being of all persons involved. If the immediate danger calls for removal of the specific items, then they should be promptly removed. If the danger is not imminent or potentially dangerous, then the appropriate authorities, such as the administration, or legal authorities, such as the police, should be notified.

It is often general hospital policy that a patient admitted through the emergency room either conscious or unconscious will have his wallet removed for identification and safekeeping. Other items of value, such as rings, clothing, etc., will either be given to family members, if present, or placed for safekeeping by hospital personnel.

The key issue here is that this limited search is permissible in a medical emergency for the purpose of ascertaining identity. The primary role of the healthcare provider is to treat the patient and give medical care. The role is not to assist the police in their investigation nor to serve as an independent investigator. This is not to say they should inhibit, obstruct, or delay appropriate legal authorities while they are doing their job. But overzealous healthcare providers have been known to step out of their roles and act inappropriately and without authority. To search citizens not under arrest at the request of a police officer could place the radiographer or healthcare provider in the position of violating a patient's constitutional rights.

Chapter 4 Disclaimer: "X-Ray Technician Should Not Have Been Terminated by Hospital for Pregnancy"

The title x-ray technician is not the proper term to identify a person that is employed in the diagnostic imaging profession. The proper title is radiologic technologist. At the time of this legal case, Alabama did not have any laws prohibiting the x-ray technician from reading films; however, the American Registry of Radiologic Technologists Code of Ethics, Principle 6, establishes that it is outside the practice standards to interpret and diagnose diagnostic images. More importantly, there are state laws, such as in California, that mandate that it is illegal for radiologic technologists to interpret images and make a diagnosis.

The article from *The Citation*, which was published by the American Medical Association, did not indicate the race of the plaintiff. Because two pregnant white female radiology technicians/radiologic technologists were not fired, it is assumed that the plaintiff was from another racial origin (nonwhite), which was in violation of the Civil Rights Act.

Glossary of Terms

Absolute right: Given to the person in whom it inheres the uncontrolled dominion over the object at all times and for all purposes.

Ad litem: For purposes of litigation.

Administrative law: Branch of law dealing with organs of government power and prescribes in the manner of their activity.

Affidavit: A declaration or statement of facts, made voluntarily, and confirmed by oath.

Age of majority: Statutory or legal age of adulthood.

Agency: Includes every relation in which one person acts for or represents another by the latter's authority.

Agent: Person authorized by another to act for him.

Appeal: A complaint to a superior court to reverse or correct an injustice done or an alleged error committed by an inferior court.

Appellate court: That court in which judgments of trial courts are reviewed or appealed.

Arbitrary: Done without adequate determining principle, not done or acting according to reason.

Arbitrator: Neutral person chosen by both sides to decide disputed issues.

Assault: Threat to do bodily harm.

Authority: Legal power, control over, jurisdiction.

Battery: Committing bodily harm.

Binding arbitration: Submission of disputed matters for final determination.

Borrowed servant: An employee temporarily under the control of another. The traditional example is that of a nurse employed by a hospital who is "borrowed" by a surgeon in the operating room. The temporary employer of the borrowed servant will be held responsible for the act(s) of the borrowed servant under the doctrine of respondeat superior.

Breach of contract: Unjustified failure to perform the terms of a contract as agreed upon or when performance is due.

Captain of the ship doctrine: Person in charge may be held responsible for all those under his supervision and makes the final decision.

Cause of action: Averment of allegations or facts sufficient to cause defendant to respond to allegations.

Civil law: Concerned with the legal rights and duties of private persons.

Civil malpractice: Professional misconduct involving a criminal act.

Client: Person who retains or employs an attorney to represent him in legal proceedings.

Common law: Derived from court decisions, judge-made law.

Comparative negligence: Doctrine of negligence of the plaintiff and defendant is compared and an apportionment of damages is made based on the acts the parties are found to have committed.

Compensatory damages: Amounts of money for proven loss.

Consent: A voluntary act by which one person agrees to allow someone else to do something. For hospital purposes, consent should be in writing, with an explanation of the procedures to be performed, so that proof of consent is easy.

Constitutional law: Branch of law dealing with organizations and functions of government.

Contract: A promissory agreement between two or more persons that create, modify, or destroy a legal relation. It is a legally enforceable promise between two or more persons to do or not to do something.

Contributory negligence: The act or omission amounting to want of ordinary care on the part of the complaining party, which, concurring with defendant's negligence, is the proximate cause of injury.

Corporate negligence doctrine: When the hospital as an entity is negligent. It is the failure of those entrusted with the task of providing the accommodations and facilities to carry out the purpose of the corporation, and the failure to follow, in a given situation, the established standards of conduct to which the corporation should conform.

Crime: An action or offense against society as a whole.

Criminal law: Deals with conduct offensive to society as a whole or to the state.

Cross-examination: Examination of a witness upon his evidence, given in chief to test its truth or credibility.

Culpability: Blamable, censurable, connotes fault.

Death: Termination of life.

Defamation: Offense of injuring another's reputation by false and malicious statements.

Defendant: In a criminal case, the person accused of committing a crime. In a civil suit, the defendant is the party against whom a suit is brought.

Deposition: An oral interrogation answering all manner of questions relating to the transaction at issue, given under oath and taken in writing before some judicial officer or attorney.

Due care: That degree of care or concern that would or should be exercised by an ordinary person in the same situation.

Due process: Certain procedural requirements to assure fairness.

Emancipated: The individual is no longer under the control of another.

Emergency: A threat to the life or health of an individual that is sudden and immediate.

Ethical malpractice: Professional misconduct considered improper or immoral by the profession as a whole.

Ethics: The science relating to moral action or moral value.

Euthanasia: Easy and painless death.

Evidentiary matter: Any species of proof, or probative matter presented by the act of the parties for the purpose of inducing belief in the minds of the court or jury as to their contention.

False imprisonment: Restraining another's freedom of movement without proper authority.

Fiduciary: Position of trust.

Foreseeability, doctrine of: Individual is liable for all natural and proximate consequences of any negligent acts to another individual to whom a duty is owed.

Guardian ad litem: A guardian appointed to prosecute or defend a suit on behalf of a party incapacitated by infancy or otherwise.

H.M.O.: Health Maintenance Organization.

Hearsay evidence: Evidence not proceeding from the personal knowledge of the witness.

Iatrogenesis: Produced inadvertently as a result of treatment by a physician for some other disorder.

Imputed: Ascribed vicariously to a person.

Indemnified: Made whole again, reimbursed.

Informed consent: One in which the patient has receive sufficient information concerning the healthcare proposed, its incumbent risks, and the acceptable alternatives.

Injunction: A court order to stop a party to the contract from performing the specific promise or act under other circumstances.

Invasion of privacy: The right to be "left alone" to live in seclusion without being subjected to unwarranted or undesired publicity.

Jurisdiction: The court has the authority to hear the case.

Law: The sum total of manmade rules and regulations by which society is governed in a formal and legally binding manner.

Legal: Permitted or authorized by law.

Liability: An obligation one has incurred or might incur through any act or failure to act; responsibility for conduct falling below a certain standard that is the causal connection of the plaintiff's injury.

Libel: Defamatory words that are printed, written, or published, which affect the character or reputation of another in that they tend to hold him up to ridicule, contempt, shame, disgrace, or to degrade him in the estimation of the community.

Litigation: A trial in court to determine legal issues and the rights and duties between the parties.

Lower court (inferior court): Court that has limited authority.

Malpractice: Professional misconduct, improper discharge of professional duties, or a failure to meet the standard of care by a professional that results in harm to another.

Mandate: Command or direction that is properly authorized and a person is bound to obey.

Medical record: A written official documentary of what has happened to a particular patient during a specific period of time.

Mitigation: Abatement or diminution of penalty imposed by law.

Moral: Normatively human, what is expected of humans, that which they ought to do.

Mutual assent: Clear understanding between or among parties considering an offer; known in law as a meeting of the minds.

Negligence: Failure to act as an ordinary prudent person, conduct contrary to that of a reasonable person under specific circumstances.

Nominal damages: Token compensation where the plaintiff has proven his case, but the actual injury or loss is not possible to prove.

Non compos mentis: Not of sound mind.

Offeree: One who accepts an offer.

Offeror: One who makes an offer.

Outrageous conduct, doctrine of: Conduct that is beyond all possible bounds of decency and is regarded as atrocious and utterly intolerable in a civilized community.

Parens patriae: Duty of the state to protect its citizens.

Perpetrator: Person who commits a crime, or by whose agency the act occurs.

Plaintiff: The party who brings a civil suit seeking damages or other legal relief.

Policies: Guidelines within which employees or an institution must operate.

Power of attorney: An instrument authorizing another to act as one's agent.

Precedent: A previous adjudged decision that serves as authority in a similar case.

Preponderance: Great weight of evidence, or evidence that is more credible and convincing to the mind.

Prima facie: So far as can be judged from the first disclosure; on the first appearance. A prima facia case is presented when all necessary elements of a valid cause of action are alleged to exist. The actual existence of such facts is then subject to proof and defense at trial.

Privileged communication: Statements made to one in a position of trust, usually an attorney, physician, or spouse. Because of the confidential nature of the information, the law protects it from being revealed, even in court.

Probate: Proving wills or handling estates.

Procedures: Mode of proceeding by which a legal right is enforced. A series of steps outlined by the institution to accomplish a specific objective or task.

Profession: The act of professing; collective body of persons in a profession.

Proximate cause: Legal concept of cause and effect; the injury would not have occurred but for the particular cause; causal connection.

Punitive damages: Money awarded as a penalty, damages relating to punishment.

Qualified right: Gives the possessor a right for certain purposes or under certain circumstances only.

Quid pro quo: Something for something.

Reasonable care: That degree of skill and knowledge customarily used by a competent health practitioner or student of similar education and experience in treating and caring for the sick and injured in the community in which the individual is practicing.

Reasonable doubt: Ordinary or usual knowledge of facts of a character calculated to induce a doubt in the mind of an ordinary intelligent and prudent person.

Reasonably prudent man doctrine: Requires a person of ordinary sense to use ordinary care and skill.

Rebuttal: Introduction of evidence to show statement of witness is not credible.

Redress: Satisfaction for the injury sustained.

Res ipsa loquitur: "The thing speaks for itself." A doctrine of law applicable to cases where the defendant had exclusive control of the thing that caused the harm and where the harm ordinarily could not have occurred without negligent conduct. Normally, the plaintiff must prove the defendant's liability, but when this doctrine is found to apply, the defendant must prove himself not responsible for the harm.

Respondeat: The person who argues against a petition or appeal, generally the person who prevailed in the lower court, the appellee.

Respondeat superior: "Let the master answer." The employer is responsible for the legal consequences of the acts of the service or employee while he acts within the scope of his employment.

Right: Power, privilege, or faculty inherent in one person and incident upon another.

Rules and regulations: Clear and concise statements mandating or prohibiting certain activity in an institution.

Sacrosanct: Not to be violated.

Sequester: Setting apart, to isolate witnesses or juries.

Signatory: One who signs.

Slander: Speaking falsely about another with resulting injury to his reputation.

Standard of care: Those acts performed or omitted that an ordinary prudent person in the defendant's position would have done or not done; a measure by which the defendant's conduct is compared to ascertain negligence.

Standard of reasonableness: Measures how the average, ordinary, prudent individual is expected to act in certain circumstances.

Standards: Criteria of measuring, and conformity to established practice.

Statue of limitations: A legal limit on the time one has to file suit in civil matters, usually measured from the time of the wrong or from the time a reasonable man would have discovered the wrong.

Statutes: Legislative enactments; act of legislature declaring, commanding, or prohibiting something.

Statutory law: Enacted by a legislative group.

Subpoena: A court order requiring one to come to court to give testimony; failure to appear results in punishment by the court.

Subpoena duces tecum: Bring the documents.

Suit: Court proceedings where one person seeks damages or other legal remedies from another. The term is not usually used in connection with criminal cases.

Superior Court: Court of the highest and most extensive jurisdiction.

Taft–Hartley Act: Enacted in 1947 by Congress, considered a promanagement law. It excluded nonprofit hospitals from federal coverage.

Tort: A legal or civil wrong committed by one person against the person or property of another.

Unit of employees: A group of two or more who share common employment interests and conditions.

Verdict: The formal declaration of the jury of its findings of fact, which is signed by the jury foreman and presented to the court.

Verdict of acquittal: Argument that there is not sufficient evidence against the defendant to proceed and the case should be dismissed.

Viability: Capability of living; term to denote the power a newborn infant possesses to exist independently.

Vicarious: Substitute.

Void: Having no legal force.

Wagner Act: First national labor relations act, enacted in 1935 to protect workers' rights to organize and elect their own representatives.

Waived: Renounced or gave up a privilege.

Witnessing: One who testifies to what he has seen, heard, or otherwise observed.

Writ: A writing issuing from a court ordering a sheriff or other officer of the law or some other person to perform an action desired by the court or authorizing an action to be done.

References and Further Readings

Akey, C. 1987a. Certification and licensure of Radiologic Technologists, Part I. *Radiologic Technology*, 58(6): 509–512.

Akey, C., 1987b. Certification and licensure of Radiologic Technologists, Part II. *Radiologic Technology*, 59(1): 55–63.

American College of Radiology. ACR tandard for teleradiology. (With permission.) Web site: http://www.med.mc.ntu.edu.tw/~somed/teletea/document/teleradiology_standard.html

American Registry of Radiologic Technologists. ARRT Rules and Regulations. Web site: http://www.arrt.org/certification/certgenelig.htm

American Society of Radiologic Technologists. Consumer Assurance of Radiologic Excellence. Web site: http://www.asrt.org/content/GovernmentRelations/CAREBill/Federal_Minimum_Standards.aspx

Asahi Metal Indus. Co. v. Superior Court, 480, U.S. 102 (1987).

Barber v. St. Francis Cabrini Hospital, Inc., 345P Second 1307 (Los Angeles Court of Appeals, May 13, 1977). Also in *The Citation*, 28: 5, October 1977.

Berlin, L. 1998. Malpractice issues in radiology: Teleradiology, *American Journal of Radiology*. 170: 1417–1321.

Berman, L., DeLacy, G., Twomey, E., Twomey, B., Welch, T., and Eban, R. 1985. Reducing errors in the accident department. *British Medical Journal*, 290(6466): 421–422.

Bienz v. Central Suffolk Hospital, 557 N.Y.S.2d, 139 (App. 1993).

Bouchard, E. 1992. *Radiology Manager's Handbook: The Business of Radiology*. Dubuque,IA: Shepherd Inc.

Buckleu v. Grossbard, 435A Second 1150 (New Jersey Supp. Court, October 14, 1981.) In *The Citation*, 44(9), February 15, 1982.

Bundy, A. L. 1988. *Radiology and the Law*. Rockville, MD: Aspen Publishers, Inc.

California Administrative Code. Title 17, Part I, Chapter 5, Subchapter 4.5, 1969. Laws relating to radiologic technology. No author, no publisher. http://ccr.oal.ca.gov/

California, Department of Fair Employment and Housing. Government Code, Section 7287.6 and 7291(f)(1) of the California Code of Regulations, Title 2, Division 4. *Sexual Harassment*. No author, no publisher. http://www.dfeh.ca.gov/publications

Call v. City of Burley, 57 Idaho 58, 62 Pac. 2d 101 (1936).

Casarella, W.J. 1996. Benefits of teleradiology. *Radiology,* 201: 16–17.

Cepelewicz, B.B. June 2003. Telelegalities. *The Journal of Imaging Technologies Management.* Web site: http://www.imagingeconomics.com/library/tools/printengine. asp?printArticleID=200306-13

Charles v. U.S., 278F. 2d 286 (1960).

Cobb v. Grant, supra, the California Supreme Court.

Creighton, H. 1981. *Laws Every Nurse Should Know,* 4th ed. Chicago: Year Book Medical Publishers.

Committee on Pediatric Emergency Medicine. March 2003. "Policy Statement: Consent for Emergency Medical Services for Children and Adolescents. *Pediatrics,* 111 (3), 703–706. http://aappolicy.aappublications.org/cgi/content/full/pediatrics;111/3/703.

Cushing, M. 1985. How a suit starts. *American Journal of Nursing,* 85(6): 655–656.

Darling v. Charleston Community Hospital, 211 N.E. Second 53 (Illinois), 1965.

DeCann, R. 1985. What is a good radiographer. *Radiography,* 51(597): 127–132.

Diana L. Webb v. T.D. & C.H.A., No. 97-255, 951 P.2d, 1008; 1997, the Supreme Court of Montana.

Doyle, E. 1991a. The fine line of the law. *RT Image,* 4(33): 3–6.

Doyle, E. 1991b. Morals in the workplace. *R.T. Image,* 4(46): 6–10.

Doyle, E., and Keefer, B. 1991. Sexual harassment: A hospital issue. *RT Image,* 4(12): 10–11.

Doyle, E. 1992. Is OSHA coming for you? *RT Image,* 6(11): 13–16.

Eckley, A.K. 1984. The role of radiology in forensic pathology. *Diagnostic Imaging,* 6(9): 145–159.

Ehrlick, R.A. and Givens, E.M. 1985. *Patient Care in Radiography.* St. Louis: The C.V. Mosby Company.

Farwell vs. Boston W.R. Corporation, 45 Massachusetts 49, 1942.

Gebhard, P.G. 1987. Securing informed consent: The radiologists responsibility. In *Medical Legal Issues for Radiologists,* (A.E. James, Ed.). Chicago: American College of Radiology, p. 114.

Gerber, P.C. 1985. Good Samaritan laws. *Physicians Management,* 25(4): 99–100, 106–107, 111.

Gonzales v. Nork, California Supreme Court, November 19, 1973

Graff, B. 1985. Anatomy of malpractice trial. *American Journal of Nursing,* 85(6): 655–656.

Greenberg v. Perkins, 845, P.2d, 530 (Colorado, 1993).

Grey, J.F., Lisk, K.G., Haddick, D.H., et al., 1985. Test pattern for video displays and hard copy cameras. *Radiology* 154: 519–527.

Gurley, L.T. and Calloway, W.J. 1986. *Introduction to Radiologic Technology.* St. Louis: Multimedia Publishing, Inc.

Hamer, M.M. 1987. Medical malpractice in diagnostic radiology. *Radiology,* 164(1): 263–266.

Hammonds v. Aetna Casualty and Surety Company (243 F. Supp. 793), Ohio, 1965.

Hanson, J. 1989. Limited licensing: Why is the ARRT involved? *Radiologic Technology,* 60(2): 168–169.

Hatfield, S. 1992. Radiology helps identify victims of bizarre killings. *Advance for Radiologic Science Professionals*, 5(8): 5.

Hays v. Shelby Memorial Hospital, 546F, Supp. Court 259 (DC, Alabama, August 18, 1982.) Also in *The Citation*, 1983, 46(8), American Medical Association.

Hemet, M. and Mackert, M. 1982. *Dynamics of Law in Nursing and Health Care*, 2nd ed. Reston, VA: Preston Publishing Company.

Horne v. Patton (287 Sa. 2nd 8242), Alabama, 1973.

Hospital Authority of Hall County v. Adams, 140 SE, Second 139 (Georgia, 1964).

Hospitals to develop policies on patient rights, euthanasia. *R.S. Wavelength*, 3(4): 3.

Hunton, B. 1993. Good communication means good patient care. *Advance for Radiologic Science Professionals* 6(9): 9.

International Shoe Co. v. Washington, 326, U.S. 310 (1945).

Keats, T. 1992. Manual labor and radiologic technology. *Applied Radiology*, 21(1): 13.

Keefer, B. 1992. Facing the risk. *RT Image*, August 10, 6(12): 12–14.

Knight, B. and Evans, K.T. 1981. *Forensic Radiology*. Oxford, London: Blackwell Scientific Publishers, August 10.

Kramer, C. 1976. *Medical Malpractice*, 4th ed. New York: Practicing Law Institute.

Kuntz, L. 1992. Piecing the past together. *R.T. Image*, 5(17): 41–43.

Landeros v. Flood (1976) Cal. 3d 399, California Supreme Court.

Leach, R.A. 1986. Technologist shortage? *Radiology Management*, 8(3): 55–56.

Lee, C.D. 1996. Teleradiology. *Radiology*. 201: 15.

Lopez v. Aziz, 852, S.W.2d, 303 (Texas App. 1993).

Malkin, L. 1992. Child abuse. *R.T. Image*, 5(16): 3–7.

Malpractice crisis: Public awareness by confused on details. 1985. *Medical World News*. 26(23): 21–22.

Mapp v. Ohio, 367 U.S. (1961).

Mays, P.S. 1986. Organization and operation of the radiology department. In L.T. Gurley and W.S. Calloway, Eds., *Introduction to Radiologic Technology*, 2nd ed. St. Louis: The C.V. Mosby Company.

McCue, P. 1988. Update on state licensing of radiologic technologists. *Applied Radiology*, 70(2): 19–21.

Nelson v. Patrick, 293 SE, Second 829 (North Carolina Court of Appeals, August 3, 1982). In *The Citation*, 46(8): 89–90, 1982.

Office for Civil Rights, *The Summary of HIPAA Privacy Rule*. Health and Human Services, Washington, D.C. Web site: www.hhs.gov/ocr/privacysummary.pdy

Orange County Register, The, Fired worker can sue understaffed hospital by Serena Maria Daniels, April 1987, p. A-3

Orphanoudakis, S.C., Kaldoudi, E., and Tsiknakis, M. 1996. Technological Advances in Teleradiology. *European Journal of Radiology*. 22: 205–207. Web site http://www.ics.forth.gr/eHealth/publications/papers/1996/telerad/telerad.html

Partida v. Park North General Hospital, 592 SW Second 38 (Texas Court of Civil Appeals, November 15, 1979.) In *The Citation*, 40(5), December 15, 1979.

Peters, J.D. 1984. Malpractice in hospitals. *Law for Medical Health Care*, 12(6): 254–259.

Plumadore v. State of New York, 427 NYS 2d 90, NY Supreme Court, Appellate Division, April 24, 1980.

Pozgar, G.D. 1987. *Legal Aspects of Health Care Administration,* 3rd ed. Rockville, MD: Aspen Publishing, Inc.

Reitherman, R. 1992. The forces behind accreditation. *Radiologic Technology,* 63(3): 203–204.

Schloendorf v. Society of New York Hospital, 211 N.Y. 125, 105 N.E. 92, 1914.

Smith v. Couter, 575, SW Second 199 (Missouri Court of Appeals, May 1, 1978). Rehearing denied, June 12, 1978; transfer denied, January 29, 1978. In *The Citation,* 33(3): 26.

Simpson v. Sisters of Charity of Providence in Oregon, 588 P Second 4 (Oregon Supreme Court, December 19, 1978).

Sivaswamy, R., et al. 2002. Doctors on the Internet: Legal and practical mplications. *Eubios Journal of Asian and International Bioethics.* 12: 185–188. Web site: http://www2. unescobkk.org/eubios/EJ125/ej125j.html

Soon, L.P. 2005. Medicolegal issues in radiology. *SMA News.* 37 (12: 7–9.

Spring, D.B., Tennehouse, D.J., Akin, S.R., and Margulis, A. 1988. Radiologists and informed consent lawsuits. *Radiology,* 156(1): 245–248.

Straub Clinic and Hospital, Inc. v. Chicago Insurance Company, 665 P2d 176 Hawaii Intermediate Court of Appeals, June 8, 1983.

Teleradiology, *Radiology,* 1996, 201: 15.

The professional status of radiologic technologists. 1990. *Radiologic Technology,* 60(3): 246–255.

Tilke, Brenda. 1995. FDA now requires RT(R)(M) or equivalent. *Advance for Radiologic Science Professional,* 8(18): 4.

U.S. Department of Health and Human Services. 1985. Standards for the Accreditation of Educational Programs for the Credentialing of Radiologic Personnel, *Federal Register,* Washington, D.C.

U.S. Department of Labor. Employment Standards Administration. Wage and Hour Division, Regulations, Part 541, WH Publication 1281, revised June 1993, Washington, D.C.

U.S. Office for Civil Rights, *The Summary of HIPAA Privacy Rule,* Department of Health and Human Services, Washington, D.C. Web site: http://www.hhs.gov/ocr/privacy-summary.pdy

Ward, J. 1985. Torts and technologists. *Educator: The Newsletter for Clinical and Staff Educators in Radiology,* 11(1): 1–2.

Warner, S. 1981. Risk management: An analysis of technologist's liability. *Radiologic Technology,* 53(6): 48–55.

Wheeler v. Yettie Kersting Memorial Hospital, 866, S.W.2d, 32 (Texas, APP. 1993).

White, P. 2002. Legal issues in teleradiology — Distant thoughts. *British Journal of Radiology,* 75: 201–206.

Wosoba v. Kenyon, 215 Iowa 226, 243 N.E. 569 (1932).

Wright v. Yackley, 459, F. 2d, 287 (9th Cir. 1972).

Ybarra v. Spangard, California Supreme Court, 1944.

Willig, S. 1977. Nurse's guide to law. New York: McGraw-Hill Publishing Company.

Wilson, B.G. 1997. Ethics and law for medical imaging professionals. Philadelphia: F.A. Davis Company.

Answers to Review Questions

Chapter 1

1. C
2. A
3. A
4. A
5. D
6. B
7. A
8. B
9. C
10. B

Chapter 2

1. B
2. D
3. D
4. D
5. A
6. D
7. C

Chapter 3

1. D
2. A
3. A
4. B
5. C
6. A
7. C
8. B

Chapter 4

1. D
2. B
3. A
4. D
5. A
6. B
7. C
8. C
9. B
10. A
11. C
12. A

Chapter 5

1. C
2. D
3. B
4. D
5. D

Chapter 6

1. B
2. B
3. A
4. B

5. D
6. B

Chapter 7

1. B
2. C
3. B
4. D
5. A
6. A

Chapter 8

1. B
2. A
3. D
4. C
5. C
6. A
7. C

Chapter 9

1. C
2. B
3. C
4. B
5. B
6. C
7. A
8. B

Chapter 10

1. D
2. A
3. B
4. C
5. D

Chapter 11

1. C
2. B
3. B
4. B

Index